Writing BETTER
FUNDRAISING
applications

A practical guide

3rd edition

Michael Norton
Mike Eastwood

DIRECTORY OF SOCIAL CHANGE

In association with the Institute of Fundraising

Published by
The Directory of Social Change
24 Stephenson Way
London NW1 2DP
tel: 020 7209 5151, fax: 020 7391 4804
e-mail: books@dsc.org.uk
from whom further copies and a full publications list are available.

The Directory of Social Change is a Registered Charity no. 800517

First published 1992
Second edition 1997
Third edition 2002

ISBN 1 903991 09 9

British Library Cataloguing in Publication Data
A catalogue record for this book is available from the British Library

Cover design by Keith Shaw

Designed by Sarah Nicholson

Typeset by GreenGate Publishing Services, Tonbridge

Printed and bound by Page Bros., Norwich

Other Directory of Social Change departments in London:
Courses and Conferences tel: 020 7209 4949
Charityfair tel: 020 7391 4860
Research tel: 020 7391 4880
Publicity tel: 020 7391 4900

Directory of Social Change Northern Office:
Federation House, Hope Street, Liverpool L1 9BW
Courses and Conferences tel: 0151 708 0117
Research tel: 0151 708 0136

CONTENTS

About the book   v

1   Introduction: what makes a good application   1
     Fundraising is selling a good idea   1
     The importance of making a good case   1
     The key steps in drawing up a proposal   2
     The function and purpose of the proposal   4
     Applications basics   5

2   The ingredients of a good application   7
     Your key selling points   7

3   Building confidence and credibility   18
     Credibility   18
     Financial credibilty   24
     Getting and using facts and figures   26
     Understanding your weaknesses   27
     Success and failure   29

4   Improving your chances   32
     Think in project terms   32
     Making a project more fundable   38
     How to develop good ideas   39
     Adding value   40

5   Costing a project   43
     The budget   43
     The budgeting process   43
     Common mistakes in budgeting   49

6   Improving your communication skills   52
     Writing in plain English   52
     Some common writer's diseases   53
     Using different media   61

7   Before you write   63
     Donor research   63

8   Writing a good application   67
     The form of the application   67
     The structure of the application   69

The length of the application   82

Back-up information   83

9   **Sending your application**   **85**

What to do with your application   85

What to do after the application   89

Timing and timescale   90

10   **Worked examples**   **92**

11   **Assessing your application**   **115**

12   **Checklists and fact files**   **122**

Further reading and sources of information   **136**

ABOUT THE BOOK

This is a practical guide on how to write a good fundraising application. It's now in its 3rd edition. Since it was first printed in 1992 many funders have come (some have gone), but the key elements of a good fundraising application remain the same. Therefore, the key elements of this book have stayed the same.

The book covers much more than the actual writing of an application. It shows you what information you will need to have available before you put pen to paper – or finger to keybaord – and how to get it. Good fundraising isn't simply about bashing out a stream of letters to possible funders. You need to build your credibility, develop good ideas, marshal the facts and figures you will need, and construct a realistic budget which will not leave you short of money at the end of the day. This book looks at all of that. It also suggests some things to do once you have sent your application off.

Writing applications is an art, not a science. There is no 'identikit' good application. What works well for one organisation, or one fundraiser, may not work for another. So if your current efforts are bringing you the desired results, there is no need to change your style or approach to match the advice given in this book. But there are general lessons which are well worth learning, and it will almost always be possible for anyone to write a better fundraising application.

A good application will not in itself lead to fundraising success. Donors want to know that you are a successful organisation, able to spend your money cost-effectively on a good project. It is your work they are paying for, not a nicely written and prettily presented proposal. But a good application is one part – and an important part – of a successful fundraising approach.

Occasionally, and this is particularly the case with grants from statutory sources and the National Lottery, you will need to complete an application form. The same principles apply as for writing an application. You simply have less freedom as you are restricted to keeping within the structure of the application form.

Finally, don't give up easily. Just because you are turned down once does not automatically mean that the application was poor, or the project is unfundable. Learn any lessons you can, but keep at it. Even the best fundraiser doesn't get money every time.

Good luck!

Michael Norton
Mike Eastwood

1 INTRODUCTION: WHAT MAKES A GOOD APPLICATION

Fundraising is selling a good idea

Fundraising is all about selling an idea to someone who has the means to help you make it happen. If you are successful, you will get the money, sponsorship, or the support in kind that you need. You have to make the donor interested in your ideas. And if they are interested enough, then they will want to help you.

There are many ways of asking. You can ask directly in person. You might make a presentation at a meeting or to a group of potential supporters. You might use the telephone (a key and vastly under-rated fundraising aid). Or you might send a written proposal – by snail mail or e-mail. You could use your website to provide back-up information and to 'sell' your cause.

In practice, the more direct and the more personal your approach, the more likely you are to be successful. One successful fundraiser for a homelessness project commented that whenever he had persuaded the potential funder to visit him at the project, he had never failed to get money from them. They saw the homeless people and the work the project was doing, and the donation followed very quickly.

The importance of making a good case

There are many ingredients in a successful fundraising approach: a good project, the impact of the work, the involvement of users, the credibility of your organisation, the individuals involved in the work, and the interest of the person being approached will all be crucial. But it is important to remember that the approach itself is an opportunity for you to make a good case, state your need and ask for support.

A good proposal may not get a bad project funded. But a poor proposal might considerably reduce your chances of success. It is important to put forward the best possible case when you have the opportunity to do so. People fail to do this surprisingly frequently – as some of the worked examples in Chapter 10 show.

By improving your proposal you will improve your fundraising effectiveness. You are more likely to raise the money your organisation needs – and you will do this with greater confidence, with less effort and at lower cost.

The key steps in drawing up a proposal

You may set out your proposal in a brief letter, or as a weighty document describing the project in great detail. You may produce a printed brochure to send out with a covering letter as part of a major appeal campaign, or you may send a direct mail approach to thousands of potential supporters.

However you plan to produce your proposal, the following are the steps you will need to take:

- develop your project idea into a form which has a greater chance of attracting support;
- identify possible sources of funds for the project. You will also need to find out as much as you can about the interests and concerns of each funder;

- understand *why* that particular funder might be interested in supporting your work. This is more than simply stating *what* you plan to do;
- outline a plan for the long-term funding arrangements of the project (if you expect it to carry on after the initial funding comes to an end);
- write your proposal for support clearly, coherently, forcefully and enthusiastically;
- identify the best person to make the approach. This will be the person who will sign the letter and be involved in any telephone follow-up and subsequent meetings;
- decide how and when to make the approach. An immediate approach may not work out best. You may wish to make preliminary contact or enter into informal discussions first, before you submit a formal proposal. The funder may also have particular requirements for the submission of applications which you will need to know;
- make the request, indicating as specifically as you can **how** and **how much** the funder might contribute.

Ten steps to success in fundraising

1 Keep the facts at your fingertips
Make sure that all the information you will need about your organisation and about the project is readily available. Back up your argument with facts and figures; don't just make assertions.

2 Build your credibility
Get yourself and your organisation known in the grants world, develop effective public relations, get (good) publicity for your work. Don't underestimate the value of just meeting donors informally and chatting. This is often when the best fundraising is done.

3 Develop grant-winning ideas
Some ideas and projects are so good that they have no difficulty in being funded. Think about your work and see if there are ideas or projects which will more easily win a grant.

4 Sort out your fundraising strategy
Think about how your organisation is to be funded over the next few years, whether this is realistic and what you need to do to put your organisation's funding on a secure basis. Think about how you intend to attract funds for the project immediately and on a continuing basis (if the project is to continue).

5 Research and identify likely grant prospects
Avoid the scatter-gun approach. Make carefully targeted approaches at a few funders rather than writing a circular letter to anybody and everybody. Cross-reference your ideas and projects with likely funders, matching their interests to your needs. Also, be sure you know which budget the money is coming from.

For example, if you are approaching a company, you could be looking for support from the donations budget, corporate PR, marketing or personnel department, or even its employee-giving or voluntary committee. Your approach will need to be adapted accordingly.

6 **Write a good proposal**

Write a clear and succinct application, making a really good case for support.

7 **Manage the application process**

Decide how and who is to contact the funding source, whether a formal proposal should be put to them right away, whether a meeting or visit could usefully be arranged, and how you can bring more influence to bear on the decision-making process. Also, should you be the person making the approach? Would it be better if it came from someone else? A colleague might have more established contacts with the funders, or a prestigious trustee or supporter may have more impact.

8 **Say 'thank you'**

If you succeed in getting a grant, note any restrictions or obligations on your part and make sure you comply with these. Say 'thank you' immediately.

9 **Keep in touch**

Maintain contact with those who are supporting you (obviously), but also with those who are not (where you feel they are or should be interested in your work). Report on your successes and continue to build your credibility with them.

10 **Go back**

Ask those who have supported you for further support next year or the year after – they have already demonstrated that they like you and what you are doing. Go back to those who have turned you down – if you feel that they should be interested. Persistence really can pay. Note any reasons given for rejection. It may be worth finding out whether there is a chance of reapplying and trying to fix up a meeting to discuss your proposals further.

The function and purpose of the proposal

When making a proposal to a funder, you will be aiming to:

1 **Raise money (or other support) for your organisation and its work**. This is obviously your number one objective.

2 **Raise as much money as you can from the particular funder you are approaching**. You will need to know what level of support the donor is likely to give, and whether you can expect and obtain a regular grant rather than just a one-off payment. If you do not raise the most you can from each funder, this is a missed opportunity – and will increase the amount of fundraising work you will have to do.

3 **Create, build and improve your relationship with the funder**. Your application should promote your organisation and its work. Whether or not you are successful, the funder will get to know more about you as a result of the approach. Good relationships are the cornerstone of effective fundraising. So even if you are not successful this time, you may have laid the ground for a successful approach in the future.

Applications basics

People often try to write an application as a means of working out what they should be doing. This is a recipe for disaster. Good preparation is the key. The more you get ready in advance, the easier and quicker you will find it to write a good proposal. Thinking, planning, discussing, budgeting, re-thinking, re-planning and re-budgeting all take time, but it is time well spent. You need to get together the following information before you send off the application.

1 Your selling points

A few key reasons why the work you are doing is important and why donors will want to support you. Remember, there is a massive difference between saying *what you are doing* and stressing *why it is important* and worth supporting.

2 Facts and figures about your work

Research, statistics or figures which will help demonstrate the importance of your cause, the extent of the need, the value of your work and the success of the methods you are using to carry out the project.

3 The credibility of your organisation

Endorsements and statements from other people which enhance the importance of your work and what you are trying to achieve. They should give the donor an increased confidence in your ability to deliver the work you are promising to do.

4 A plan and budget for your project

You need to be clear what you intend to do, how and when you intend to do it, and what the benefits will be. These can be written up into a simple project plan. You can then put together a financial plan for what you propose, properly and fully costed and covering all the items of expenditure you plan to incur. This should also include any income you expect to generate from the project.

5 Donor research

Find out what the funder is interested in and the scale of support you might expect (i.e. what to ask for), and identify any connections between you and the funder (personal contacts, previous approaches for support, previous meetings, etc.).

6 Back-up literature

Have brochures, annual reports, case studies of success and other good information available to attach to your written proposal. These will enhance your case and improve your chances of success.

Now you are ready to start writing your application.

The ingredients of a successful application

- Your key selling points
- Facts and figures
- Credibility and endorsements
- Project plan and budget
- Donor research
- Back-up literature
- A well-argued case

Advice and ideas on all these points are given in the following chapters.

2 THE INGREDIENTS OF A GOOD APPLICATION

Your key selling points

Most major funders receive thousands of applications each year, some as many as 30,000. Yours has to catch their attention and stand out of the pile as something worth supporting.

You need to do more than tell them what you plan to do. You have to tell them why your work is important and why it makes sense for them to support you.

You will need to make a number of key points which catch the reader's attention, arouse interest and 'sell' the proposal. For example, what is unique, special and different about the work you are doing? Why is it necessary and important? What will it achieve? What will grab the interest or excitement of a funder? Why would they want to give you money to do it?

You have limited space to get these points across, and you need to use the space effectively. Deciding the key points that you will make will help you do this.

You should try to tell people why your work is important, not just what you do.

Fundraising is much more than just asking for money. Fundamentally, it is about change. You the fundraiser need to persuade the donor that you can change things for the better. They will give you money on the expectation of change.

So how do you do all of this? Here are some of the points you might consider making.

1 The problem and the need

Voluntary organisations exist to meet important needs (for example elderly people being isolated and neglected; young people at risk of crime or abuse; disabled people being discriminated against; the environment being destroyed by overuse and pollution).

> Fundraising is about change rather than money.

Organisations must believe in what they do, enthuse about their achievements and successes. If you can't be clear and enthusiastic about the work you are doing, a potential funder certainly won't be. You must define the problem in words they can understand and in a way that makes them feel they want to do something about it. If you can't show why it is really important that your work continues and develops, you will not get the money.

Try not to generalise. Many applications simply make bland assertions such as 'we work with young people excluded from school' or 'everybody knows that we have a serious drugs problem amongst young people and the problem is growing'. You need to do much more than this. You need to show the following:

- **What is the nature of the problem you are tackling?**
  For example, 'More and more young people are developing long-term health problems through lack of exercise'.
- **How widespread is it?**
  You need evidence for your claims. For example, 'Over 50% of children aged 11–16 watch more than three hours of television each night. Only 5% regularly do more than four hours physical exercise each week'.
- **Why is it important?**
  Don't assume that the reader understands the problems you are describing. Spell it out to them. Stress the importance of what you are doing and why something must be done now. If you can't, the funder may prefer to turn to someone else who can. For example, 'Already health specialists are warning that this level of inactivity at an early age is storing up serious heart problems for the future. Indeed, as a leading cardiologist recently said: ...'.
- **What are the consequences of the problem or need, and what will happen if nothing is done?**
  Show how the situation will get worse and worse as the problem grows more acute. For example, 'The surgical costs alone are expected to double to over £X million a year. This does not take account of the economic costs of increased absence from work owing to ill health'.

- **Are there any social trends which demonstrate that the problem will increase in the next few years?**

  Prevention is usually cheaper than cure; it is certainly preferable. So, if you can show how changes in society are likely to make the situation worse, these will add weight to your argument. For example, 'If people do not develop the capacity to take exercise early in life, they can effectively be cutting out a whole series of leisure options later on. As people retire earlier this could have a serious impact on their quality of life in retirement because …'.

- **What kind of people will be helped as a result of your work, and why are their needs particularly important?**

  If you have not made it clear already, describe clearly who will benefit and in what way they are disadvantaged (for example through poverty, ill health, disability, lack of facilities).

Exercise: Ask yourself the following questions

1 What are the needs of our users? (*If you're not getting anywhere, try to describe the difficulties or challenges a typical user may be having to face.*)
2 What will happen to them if we don't do anything?
3 Can we prove this?
4 What will happen to them if we do something?
5 How can we demonstrate this?

If you are a local project, you will also need to answer the following question:

- **What are the particular features of your area or community that make it specially important to give you support?**

  Not all communities are the same. Why is the need great in your area (for example no-one else is doing anything, you have a particularly high percentage of young people excluded from school, or whatever)?

Try to answer all these questions. Be as specific as you can. Give facts and figures wherever possible. Do not make generalisations or use hollow phrases such as '*urgent problem*' or '*desperate need*'. One or two key statistics can do more for your case than a page of well-intentioned waffle.

Also, and crucially, all the above is about the people you are trying to help, not about the needs of your organisation. So many people apply because '*we need a minibus*' or '*we need a new building*'. At this stage, don't talk about your own needs, stress the needs of your intended users or beneficiaries. Show what difference you (with the help of the funder) can make to their lives.

2 Your proposal

It is not enough to convince the funder that there is a real and urgent need to be met; you also need to show them that you have a sensible and practical solution to the problem. Again, you should be enthusiastic. Try to excite the donor by showing that something positive and effective can be done. Some ways of doing this are listed below.

- **State clearly what you are going to do**

  Don't just say: '*We will work with the relevant agencies to encourage young people to become more active at an early age*'. How are you going to do this? You need to be specific. For example – and continuing with the health risk example above – you could say: '*We will develop a series of basic training programmes that any young person will be able to follow. It will only require 15 minutes exercise, three days a week. Many can be done alongside existing day-to-day activities*'.

- **How can you guarantee that it will work?**

  You can't! However, you can show what practical steps you will be taking to ensure that there is every chance of success. So: '*Local celebrities – including X Olympic champion – will visit every school and youth club in the area to talk to children about the health risks they run without proper physical exercise. They will hand out the basic training programmes and do a demonstration exercise with the children. They will follow this up with repeat visits to the schools and clubs. We will also run activity sessions in school holidays in which …*'.

  Funders are – or at least appear to be – increasingly risk averse. The more that you can reassure them that you have the capacity to deliver the intended benefits of the work, the more likely they are to fund you. This is one key reason why so many funders now ask about your management committee. They want to know that the management committee has a good range of professional skills, or if not then it knows good people to turn to for help and advice.

  Funders don't like to appear to fail. The excellence of your people, their experience of this kind of work, your organisation's overall track record – these are all important factors in convincing the funder that their money will be well spent through you.

- **How will you measure success?**

  Many grant-makers now view 'output funding' – where they gauge the success of the project on the measurable things it achieves – as another basic element of the grant-making decision. What targets are you going to set for the project? Or, as the National Lottery Community Fund puts it: '*Describe between one and three benefits that will result each year from this project. How will you know if the project is delivering these benefits and meeting its overall aim?*'

Again, to use the above example: *'Our project will visit each school in the area three times a year; we will visit each youth club at least once a year. This means we will speak to W thousand children and hand out X thousand training programmes. Based on our previous pilot study, we expect Y hundred to attend at least one of our school holiday activity sessions. And anybody who successfully completes level 8 of the programme will get a certificate personally signed by .... We aim to present Z hundred of these certificates at schools and youth clubs each year.'*

Try to give the funder a clear plan of action, including numbers involved, where, when and how it will all happen.

3 The involvement of users

It is increasingly important to show funders that your users, the people who will benefit from the work you are trying to get funded, are committed to the ideas you are putting forward. Funders do not like the idea that your users are being 'done to', that you know what's best for them. Rather, they want to see that your users have been fully involved in helping shape the project plans. This can be done in a number of ways:

- **The involvement of users and ex-users in running the organisation**. Do you have users or former users on your management committee? If not, do you have people who can speak with real knowledge and sympathy on behalf of the users, aside from paid members of staff?
- **The involvement of users and ex-users in running the programme**. Will users work or volunteer on the project? Will they be part of the project steering group? Can you prove that the kind of people who will be benefiting from the work of the project will also have a say in how it is delivered?
- **The involvement of users in drawing up and planning the project or in the management of the organisation**. Show that you don't know best and that you are not trying to impose your ideas, but that the plans and ideas have come from those who really know – your users. This can be done through user groups, questionnaires, community surveys and such like.

To quote from the Community Fund assessment manual under the section on beneficiaries being involved in developing the project: *'Were potential beneficiaries [users] among those first involved in developing the plans for the project, and have they been as it has been elaborated? If beneficiaries were not directly involved, were they directly consulted for their views?'* Community Fund users – quite rightly – are at the centre of the planning process; they are not, and never should be, simply an afterthought. Make sure you can prove that your users – or at least their representatives – are fully committed to the project your are proposing.

4 Your effectiveness and cost-effectiveness

Most funders are vastly over-subscribed and could easily spend their money many times over on the basis of the applications they receive. You need to show that you represent a good investment, that money spent on your project gives maximum benefit for an appropriate cost. There are a number of ways in which you can do this:

- **Can you demonstrate that your work is effective?**

  Have you got a good track record? Have you gone from strength to strength? Or at least, have you done one thing really well? Can you show that you have achieved real results before? If so, what were they and why were they so great? Can you get a supportive quote from someone that the funder will respect?

  In fundraising terms, success breeds success. Indeed, many funders, when considering your application, ask themselves: '*What does the history of this organisation say about its likely future?*' If you simply lurch from crisis to crisis, they may well assume that you will never be able to work effectively and efficiently. If you are constantly in debt, they will loathe to risk their money on you. However, if you have a track record of breaking even each year, of receiving and managing grants well, of delivering good quality and well-valued work, they will take great confidence from all this and your application will be all the stronger as a result.

- **Can you show that what you plan to do is an efficient and cost-effective way of dealing with the problem?**

  How many people will be helped? How many will use the facilities? And at what cost per person and with what results? Ideally, you should be able to show high numbers at low cost. For example, '*The schools pack will only cost £5,000 to produce but will be used by over 20,000 young people over the next three years*'.

  Funders like to know exactly what will happen as a result of their giving money – how many people will be helped, by whom and when. These kinds of outputs are increasingly important in persuading funders that your ideas are well thought through and, by implication, more effective.

- **What will be the outcome of your work?**

  Outcomes are what happens as a result of your work – not just what you do, but the impact this has and the changes that take place. For example, in an employment training project, it is not just the number of people trained that is important, but the number of people who get proper employment as a result – and the number that continue to be in employment after a year.

The three Os

Many funders talk in terms of objectives, outputs and outcomes.

- The objective is the aim of the project, what you are trying to achieve (e.g. 'we are aiming to provide a mobile welfare rights advice service giving specialist advice to low-income families in their own home')
- The outputs are what and how much gets delivered (e.g. 'we aim to provide 25 advice sessions a week')
- The outcomes are the difference your work will make in the short and long-term (e.g. 'we aim to help people lead more independent lives as they take control over their own income and financial planning')

Make sure that you are clear about the aims, outputs and outcomes of your project. This will reassure funders that you are a well managed, well thought-through outfit who would use their money effectively.

- **Does your work represent value for money and does it compare well (or better) to alternative approaches to dealing with the problem?**
  Showing value for money is increasingly important, especially to trusts and the National Lottery Community Fund. They want to make sure that they are getting the maximum benefits from the money they spend.

  You could show how much money will be saved as a result of your work. For example, drug-related crime costs £X per week and you get, on average, five people a year off drugs. This will reduce the cost of crime by £Y. Alternatively, you may stop people turning to crime; you may prevent environmental decay; you may stop people staying away from school; you may prevent people having to have expensive medical treatment. You can put a cash value on all of these savings.

  You could try to show how your work brings lasting benefits to your users and their families and then put a value on these benefits. For example, if you help people acquire new skills they will have these skills for life, plus they may well be more confident in other areas as a result. They will become more employable, and this may turn them from being benefit recipients into tax payers.

  You could try to show that by spending money you will generate money. Your advice sessions costing £X may result in several hundred people receiving £Y in unclaimed benefits; you may help people save money on heating bills; you may be able to develop a service that you can charge for which will underpin your organisation's financial security. Again, you are showing how a small amount of money given to you now leads to a long-term benefit well in excess of the value of the grant given.

Knowing the effectiveness, the impact and the cost-effectiveness of your work can help you make a good case. It will also help you manage your project better. Monitoring and evaluation are an important aspect of your work. If you can demonstrate success, people will want to support you.

Not everything has to be done at the lowest cost. You need to balance the quality with the quantity of your output. If you are dealing with special needs which require particular effort, or if you are doing more than just papering over the problem, then this too can be made explicit and turned into a point in your favour. Show how you are getting to the heart of the problem that everyone else is ignoring while the cost of the neglect just grows and grows. However, if your work appears 'expensive', make sure you explain why this is still the lowest realistic cost for meeting this really important need.

Selling points: an example

A local youth club will highlight different selling points when appealing to different donors. For example:

1 To the local authority

- You deliver their strategic objectives for young people (e.g. personal development work, diversionary activities for young people at risk).
- You run a 'professional' service using qualified leaders and meeting all technical and other requirements. Previous club members are now trained leaders.
- You are efficient – you attract the correct ratio of young people to session leaders or staff.
- You have excellent child protection procedures.
- You are effective – you run an excellent service.
- There is a need – your catchment area has a high incidence of need and a low provision compared with other areas.
- You lever in support from other sources.
- You are cost-effective and provide value for money.

2 To the parents of local young people

- You provide a 'containment service', keeping young people off the streets and out of harm's way.
- You provide an educational service – your programme of activities is attractive, and young people acquire new skills and interests.
- You take young people to places they otherwise would not be able to get to, or they undertake activities they have never done before.
- You do all this at extremely low cost – only a few pounds per term.

3 To grant-making trusts

- There is a real need and only you are meeting it.
- Your work is well thought of and you have achieved maximum possible funding from statutory sources.
- The project you are proposing is an interesting development or an innovative approach to dealing with a particular problem. If successful, other groups elsewhere could copy it.
- You are using new media (e.g. arts, sport, IT) for engaging with young people and the particular trust has an interest in this.
- Other trusts have supported you and are continuing to support you.

4 To local companies

- You are keeping people off the streets and from doing harm. The company may then have a vested interest in supporting them on these grounds!
- There are educational, training, work experience benefits, all of interest to companies. Ultimately this will bring them high quality recruits.
- You are a well-run and successful local charity, so it makes sense for them to support you out of a sense of local community responsibility.
- Children of company staff are or have been youth club members; current leaders are company employees.
- The company will get good publicity in the local press in return for the donation – and you can show evidence that you have obtained such publicity before.

4 Other plus points

There are a whole range of other key points that you may wish to make.

- **Your use of volunteers**. Time is precious. If people willingly give you some of theirs this must be a point in your favour. You may also be giving volunteers transferable skills and training opportunities as well as saving the cost of having to pay people to do the work.
- **Your ability to mobilise support in kind**. Show that you can think around a problem, that you are not just cash-obsessed.
- **Your ability to attract support from other sources**, and particularly from the statutory sector.
- **Your financial security** and **sustainability** in the medium and long-term. Show that you are a safe bet.
- **The proportion of funds you generate** or propose to generate yourselves. Self-help at every level is very attractive to funders.
- **The support you get in membership or donations** from the local community. Having community support is another strong plus point.

- **Collaboration with other organisations**. Show how you avoid unnecessary duplication and overlap, and that between you you provide a comprehensive service.
- **Leverage** – that is being able to demonstrate how a large impact can be produced from a relatively small amount of support. You can also show the grant will be used to mobilise further support.

All these will be seen as plus points by funders. They will show you as resourceful and effective, and show funders that their pounds will be well 'invested' with you, creating, as the Americans say, *'more bang for the buck'*.

You must be able to come up with several good reasons why your project should be supported. You need to make these the key 'selling points' in your proposal. You may well not be able to get all of them into every application. Rather, highlight those that are the most important as well as those that are of specific interest to that particular donor.

It is a good idea to work out what your key selling points are, and then to discuss and agree them with your colleagues and your management committee or trustees. These points will be the basis on which you present your organisation when you are seeking support, so it is important that they reflect how people within the organisation see the organisation and its work.

If there is anything you are unhappy with where you feel that the organisation could be doing better, this is something that you should raise with the organisation. Anyone trying to raise money for an organisation must believe that the organisation is doing the best job it can and, if there are problem areas – as there often are – that it is doing its best to sort these out.

Exercise: Your selling points

Try to write down at least three selling points under each of the following headings. Ask other people in the organisation for their ideas too.

We meet the following need(s):

The needs we meet are particularly important because:

The following shows that we are effective:

We are different or unique because:

Our other strengths are:

If we did not exist then:

Funders usually prefer to support successes rather than failures. Therefore, you need to be able to show a track record of successes. List your five greatest successes in recent years (e.g. in the past three years).

1

2

3

4

5

If you get stuck, complete the following sentence:

We are the best because…

3 BUILDING CONFIDENCE AND CREDIBILITY

Credibility

Fundraising is as much who you know (and who knows you) as what you do. Indeed, it is sometimes said that fundraising is 10% what you know and 90% who you know. The figures may not be that extreme, but it is important to know and be known. Organisationally you need to be known, liked and trusted. It also helps if you are personally known, liked and trusted.

Some professional grant-makers may have heard of you well before you have even discovered them. It is their business to know what is happening and to identify the successful projects, organisations and individuals that are making things happen. However, don't just wait for them to find you. It is your business to get yourself noticed and to establish your reputation. Funders support you because they believe in you and your organisation's ability to run good projects, as much as in the specific project for which you are seeking funds.

Sometimes funders will support you because they have heard about what you are doing and believe in the cause, sometimes because they have come into contact with you, sometimes because of a personal contact or commendation, sometimes because they have heard of the patrons, trustees or prominent people associated with you. All of this can be as important as the quality of work you are doing and the excellence of your written proposal.

Assume that a funder agrees that you have demonstrated a clear and important need and that you have a sensible plan for dealing with the problem. Their next question is: *'That's all very well, but how can I trust this lot to deliver on this?'* In many ways this is the key question. There are lots of good ideas around. You need to show that you have a good idea and the ability to make it happen. You can do this by showing how good and clear your solutions to the problem are. However, you also need to establish your credibility.

You need to show that you have ability and profesionalism, that you have support in the community and that you have a track record of success.

Credibility for new organisations

Credibility generally comes with your good track record, but if you are new – or relatively new – you don't really have one. So what can new organisations do to demonstrate their credibility?

- Talk about the expertise of all those involved in the work.
- Show what excellent ideas and solutions you have to the problems you were set up to deal with.
- Show the calibre of people you have as staff, management committee members, patron, vice presidents, project advisory group or whoever.
- Get letters of support and endorsement from a range of key people and agencies.
- Demonstrate by the quality of your business and project planning that you have seen a clear need, are capable of delivering an effective solution and have thought through a sensible and clear funding plan into the long term.
- Show that the project is based on a successful model developed elsewhere, although you have modified it slightly to adapt to the particular circumstances you face.
- Try and get some early press coverage about why the project is needed and what you hope to achieve.

All you are trying to do is give the funder the confidence that you know what you want to do and how you want to do it, that other people think it's worthwhile, and that you are confident of succeeding. Doing some or all of the above should ensure you achieve this.

Your ability and professionalism

Show that you are a well-run outfit, that you have grown and developed over the years, that you are soundly financed, that you have a wide support base, that you have qualified and committed staff, that you support your volunteers with appropriate training or whatever. The days of the enthusiastic amateur are by no means over (and hopefully never will be); but the days of the incompetent amateur are numbered.

The National Lottery Community Fund assessors are told to find out whether:

- **The expertise of the trustees and staff is commensurate with the size of the organisation**. For instance, do the staff and/or the management committee have sufficient and relevant management skills? What are the backgrounds of key trustees and staff?
- **There are clear lines of reporting and supervision between committee and executive staff and volunteers**. For instance, is there a clear reporting structure – set out as an organisational chart – that specifies responsibilities for the project and the organisation. Is it clear that the project is not in the hands of one dominant individual?
- **The organisation is well-managed, with policies and financial controls appropriate to its size**. For instance, how does the committee meet, and is this adequate? Is the committee aware of its legal responsibilities (such as employment and health and safety) and does it have suitable policies in place? Are the financial controls sufficient to monitor income and expenditure and to guard against fraud?

This is all pretty tough stuff. However, funders are becoming more and more exacting about levels of risk. You need to show that you are a safe bet.

Your support in the community

Show how you have widespread support and goodwill throughout the community. Their support will strenghten your efforts and create a sense of 'ownership' in what you are doing. Also, show how your users think really well of your work – and how you involve them in the planning and delivery of your services.

Exercise: List your successes

List six recent successes in your organisation. Get other people in the organisation *(project workers, trustees, the accountant, a committed volunteer)* to list six – do the lists match up?

1
_____

2
_____

3
_____

4
_____

5
_____

6

Your track record

Show that you have successfully done similar work in the past, or that you have set up other projects which have gone really well. Show how well you have been able to spend grants you have received in the past. Again, what does the history of your organisation say about its likely future? Does it show that there is nothing unusual in you applying for and receiving funding, spending it well and continuing to develop new and interesting solutions to your users' problems? If this is the case, then the funder will take great confidence from this.

Here are some things you can do:

1 Get comments and commendations from users and experts

- **Keep copies of any letters** you receive from grateful clients and users. Use selected parts to make up a 'quotes sheet' where a range of people say really positive things about you.
- **Evaluate your work**, either internally or through a formal external evaluation, and make a note of the key points from the evaluation which enhance your credibility.
- **Ask experts** and others to visit you, and then ask them to write to you with their impressions of your work. Then ask them if you can use selected quotations to endorse your work.

2 Get written about or reported in the local, specialist or national press or media

- **Keep copies of any press coverage**. If you are a national organisation you may want to use a press cuttings agency to send you copies of any coverage you receive.
- **Circulate copies** (or a collage) of the press coverage you have received to your supporters, potential supporters and key contacts where you think they will be interested.
- **Alert supporters** to forthcoming media coverage, especially TV programmes and radio phone-ins, and try to ensure that your voice is heard.
- **Tape (or videotape) any radio or TV coverage** you get. It may prove useful as part of a presentation.

3 Keep in touch with existing donors

- **Say 'thank you' promptly** for any support you have received. The most cost-effective form of fundraising is to keep hold of the supporters you already have. Research suggests that it is 11 times more expensive to get a new donor than it is to keep a current one. It is surprising how often recipients of grants fail even to thank their donors. And if you forget to, it can completely ruin your chances of getting further support. Remember, you are trying to create an on-going relationship rather than periodically scrounge for money.

- **Send progress reports** and a **final report** on the project. Some of this you may be obliged to do under the terms of your grant. Try to show what you have been able to achieve with their money – outcomes as well as outputs, and the impact you are having on the lives of individuals.
- **Build an informal working relationship with your main donors**. If you are at the same conference, go up and introduce yourself. If there is anything you need to know or want to discuss, telephone them – but don't waste their time.
- **Ensure that all queries and correspondence are answered promptly** and that telephone calls are received competently and cheerfully.
- **Suggest a visit** if they are in the area, or invite them to an 'open day' or other similar event. And then make sure that the organisation shows itself at its best.
- **Send copies of your annual report**, and any other literature you produce which you feel will be of interest, even though you are not asking for money now. You want to try and show the funder that you are committed to building a long-term relationship with them rather than simply asking for money when the last lot has run out.

4 Get known to potential funders

Much of the above is also relevant to building relationships with potential funders – those people who you believe might be interested in your work and in supporting it now or in the future. Often it will be far better to develop your credibility with potential funders before approaching them for support. This means you need to get together a target list now. This will include all those you expect to apply to over the next few years. Put them on the list to receive your annual report, press cuttings you circulate, invitations to your annual general meeting or evening receptions, or whatever seems appropriate.

When you first contact them on this basis, explain that you are not asking for money now, but that you hope they will be interested in your work and that they might be interested in supporting you at some point in the future. This does two things:

- **acts as a point of reference** when you actually get round to asking for money;
- **shows that you are committed to some sort of partnership**. You are not one of those who simply asks for cash and is not heard from again until you want more.

You never know, you may even spark an interest in the funder which encourages them to approach you or even offer you money!

5 Know who your contacts are

You may well have a lot of contacts with the trustees or administrators of funding sources, yet you may not be aware of the extent of these. Draw up a list of potential funding sources and discuss the list with your staff, your trustees, your patrons and other prominent supporters. Find out who knows whom and discuss with them how best such contacts might be mobilised in your support.

6 Bring people into your organisation

You can bring new people into your organisation, people you feel will be useful to you:

- as **patrons, vice-presidents**
- as **expert advisers**
- on to **specialist subcommittees** (events, fundraising etc.)
- as **trustees**.

You need such people as much for their contacts and to enhance your fundraising credibility, as for the practical help they can give you. Someone with good contacts can save you hours and hours of painstaking reputation-building. So if you want to raise money from local business, try recruiting a prominent and popular local businessperson and get them to ask on your behalf (as long as you make it quite clear to them from the start that this is what they are expected to do).

7 Build your credibility into your fundraising proposals

- **State on your letterhead who your patrons, trustees** and other prominent people associated with you are.
- **Mention major support or sponsorship received** (particularly from government sources and other trusts and companies). If they have supported you, this shows that you are well-regarded.
- Use **impartial comments and commendations** from users and **mention any press or media** coverage in your proposal (or as an attachment to the written application). These show others endorsing what you are doing.
- **Mention your achievements** and your successes.

8 Keep a credibility fact file

Buy a box file to keep all the press cuttings, the commendation letters and endorsements, etc. that you use in your fundraising proposals.

See also Worksheets 2 and 3 – Credibility fact file and Credibility box file – in Chapter 12.

Exercise: Estimating the value of non-cash support

For last year, estimate the following:

Value of items donated in kind

item	replacement cost
	£
	£
	£
	£
Total	£

Value of volunteer time

number of volunteers:

total hours of volunteer time valued on an hourly basis: £   per hour

total value of volunteer time: £

Remember to include all the volunteer inputs into your organisation. You can value volunteer time at the average wage, the minimum wage, the estimated cost of paying for the time or some notional – but reasonable – figure.

Value of secondments

valued on a similar basis to volunteers

NB: Were gifts in kind, volunteer time or secondments mentioned in your last year's annual accounts? Do they represent a significant proportion of your last year's total income? If the answer to the first question was no and the second question yes, what are you going to do about it?

Financial credibility

You must show that your organisation is secure, solvent and makes good use of its funds. Your accounts, which many donors require a copy of, can give hidden messages, such as:

- you are **flush with funds** or running a huge surplus, so you don't really need the money;

- you are **out of financial control**, with expenditure consistently exceeding income, so you can't be trusted with money;
- you are **spending too much on fundraising**, administration or travel, wasting the money you are given.

You may have a qualified auditor's report, saying that the accounts do not present a true and fair view of your financial position (in the auditor's opinion). This can be a disaster and you may need to explain the situation and what you are doing about it.

On the other hand, your financial accounts may not fully reflect the extent of your work. This will particularly be the case if you receive a good deal of support in kind or through the efforts of volunteers. These inputs may not be included in the financial accounts, and yet this support is important.

If your accounts (as they are currently presented) will make the work of fundraising more difficult, you will need to do something about this before you start. It may often only be a matter of presentation, getting your accountant or auditor to agree to present the figures in a different way, to set aside provisions for future expenditure, or to add explanatory notes to the accounts. Or there may be a more fundamental problem which you will need to address before you can seriously begin the task of fundraising.

However, fundamentally, funders want to know that you can handle money well. Again, to quote the excellent Community Fund assessors' manual:

- **The accounts or income projections suggest that the organisation's financial position is reasonably stable and healthy**. For instance, is the financial statement clear about the financial position? Is the organisation solvent? Are any deficits adequately explained (and under control)? Are other sources of income secure? Are any free reserves acceptable or explained?
- **Are there sufficient management controls in place (or planned) to manage the additional funds?** For instance, would the grant dramatically increase the organisation's annual income? If so, will they be able to cope, whether through existing or planned systems, or through support from other agencies?

An increasingly important aspect of financial credibility is your approach to reserves. Reserves are simply money in the bank (or invested elsewhere) that you can spend on any part of the charity's work or development. A reasonable level of reserves is now seen as a sign of good management, of taking sensible precautions in an increasingly volatile charity world. Most organisations aim to have at least the equivalent of three months' income as reserves.

Exercise: Judging your financial credibility

Get hold of a copy of your organisation's latest annual accounts. Study carefully the *Income and Expenditure Account*, the *Balance Sheet* and the *Notes to the Accounts*. Jot down some of the positive and negative points that emerge from these figures.

On the plus side:

On the minus side:

Main problem areas to explain:

Many funders now ask to see your Reserves Policy. This is a simple statement (usually up to 2 sides of A4) which addresses four basic questions:

- Why do we need reserves (e.g. to guard against financial problems and to invest in the organisation's development)?
- What level of reserves is appropriate for us (for example free reserves equivalent to 3 months' income – or perhaps more)?
- How are we going to build up a reserve within this policy (e.g. by allocating £20,000 of our annual surplus to our reserves for the next three years)?
- How will we monitor our progress (for example through scrutiny by the finance sub-committee, and including a statement in our annual accounts)?

Getting and using facts and figures

It will always be helpful to be able to illustrate the strength of your case by using facts and figures rather than making generalised statements such as '*there is a desperate need*' or '*the problem has increased dramatically in recent years*'. It is far better to show exactly how great the need is or how fast the problem has been increasing. Indeed, many funders now require hard information rather than your opinions or assertions.

Facts and figures should be objective. Try not to allow the prejudiced funder to think '*Well, they would say that, wouldn't they?*'. Get information from impartial sources, and use this to make your case for you.

A couple of choice facts can be far more effective than two paragraphs of argument. For example, a survey in an area of North West England showed that women who have been physically abused by their partners had to go, on average, to eight different agencies before they could get meaningful help. In two lines you have demonstrated an absolute and irrefutable need for a better system.

Don't assume that the facts and figures will speak for themselves. You may need to explain what the statistics mean, why your area has a higher incidence than the national average, why there is a growth in the level of need, why any changes are important, and so on.

Facts and figures are obtainable from a variety of sources:

- **Local and central government reports and surveys**, local health authority reports, reports of parliamentary Select Committees, the National Audit Office, etc.
- **Official government statistics** such as the 2001 Census data, and the annual Population Trends, Social Trends, Regional Trends and the General Household Survey.
- **A variety of other publications** including reports by special interest groups and campaigns (for example The Joseph Rowntree Foundation, Child Poverty Action Group, Cancer Research Campaign, King's Fund).
- **Your own researches** (for example questionnaires to your users, clients, potential users, your local community).
- **Academic research** published in journals and books.

Understanding your weaknesses

'Imagine the following situation: a church member comes to you and says she'd like to open a creche for working mothers. She's put together a rota of willing volunteers to staff it and there is an obvious need for such a service within the congregation. It will pay for itself and the rooms she wants are not required for any other purpose. Could you come up with half a dozen reasons why it's totally impractical? If so, you could be just the person we're looking for to be our next CHURCH WARDEN.' (From *A Survivors' Guide to the Church*)

A common reaction by someone reading your proposal is to think up all the reasons why they should reject it. Some typical reasons might be:

'There are too many charities already doing the same thing, and we are already funding *** charity.'

'I've never been to … (somewhere in the sticks – or the North!) … and I don't see why we should be spending our money there.'

'I've never heard of them so they can't be doing a very good job.'

'They have run up a huge deficit. I don't see why we should continue to pour money into them.'

'They spend far too much on administration and fundraising.'

'They are extremely rich; they have enormous assets and reserves. So they don't need our help.'

'They are an expensive service. I think we could spend our money more wisely elsewhere.'

'I remember the bad publicity when two members of their management committee resigned.'

'Their work is extremely controversial.'

'They are too political' (meaning they campaign a lot or are too left wing).

You need to be aware of the potential problems or difficulties people may raise about your organisation. Different donors will be concerned about different things. For example, a company may be looking for a clean image, whereas a grant-making trust and the National Lottery Community Fund will want to know that they are not paying for a lost local authority grant. You need to get inside the minds of the donors and address their concerns accordingly.

When you look at your organisation and its weaknesses, there may well be a perfectly good explanation for most of the apparent problems. You then have to decide whether to confront the issue head on, by mentioning the 'problem' and giving an explanation in your proposal, or whether just to be prepared with a satisfactory answer if you are ever asked a question about it. It is not very sensible simply to forget that the 'problem' exists.

Often, your fundraising is done through letter with supporting materials. There is usually no meeting and no opportunity to discuss things in more detail at a later stage. Therefore, it is usually best to try and neutralise any of the possible objections within the letter. This requires careful writing. You do not want to be as clumsy as to say: 'you [the funder] might be thinking "gosh this is really expensive". Let me show you how is isn't.' Rather, you explain that the cost of dealing with the problem is X. This is much more cost-effective than the conventional Y approach, and is certainly much cheaper than the Z cost of not doing anything at all. Or that you are dealing with a particularly vulnerable group or intractible problem, which requires much more effort to succeed. Or, if you have been running a deficit and therefore appear financially weak and generally badly managed, show how this year you will break even and next year you will even move into surplus. You could explain, for example, that the deficits were a necessary outcome of important structural changes you made, that the organisation is now much stronger and how the project you are writing about is central to the organisation's on-going development and financial viability.

Sometimes, you may have to delay your application until you have resolved some of your problems. Or at least you may need to bring them to the attention of your management committee and get them to sanction a course of action. You can then show the funder how you are already on the road to sorting out the problem.

With the National Lottery Community Fund you need to be particularly aware of your apparent failure to meet their assessment criteria. For example, they take equal opportunities and user involvement very seriously. If you cannot show user involvement in your work – and especially the project you are trying to get money for – you will reduce your chances of success. Therefore, you will need to adopt strategies to demonstrate that although you have been historically weak in the area of user involvement, you are now taking the issue very seriously. You can then show how all future projects, especially those to be funded by the Community Fund, will match their desired criteria. At least with the Community Fund you have the assessment stage to make these points. But part of their applications game is pre-guessing where they will mark you down, and showing them that by the time this new project gets going you will be well on the way to meeting their concerns.

If there are problems – especially when these will be apparent to the funder – explain what they are and show how you are already moving towards a solution. Don't just pretend they don't exist.

Success and failure

Nothing succeeds like success! Funders like to back winners, not losers. If you can demonstrate a track record of success, this is likely to improve your fundraising chances.

What do you think are your real successes and achievements over the last two or three years which could usefully lend credibility to a fundraising application?

- Successes relating to the organisation as a whole?
- Successful projects, successful events, successful work?
- Individual case study examples of success (suitably disguised if confidentiality is required)?
- Success in attracting support or sponsorship?
- Objectives that have been achieved?

Learn from failure

Although everyone wants to be successful, even the best-run organisations fail from time to time. Sometimes the project is experimental and simply does not work. Perhaps circumstances or needs will change. Occasionally a grant will be cut or further funding will fail to materialise. Sometimes it is due to circumstances beyond your control.

Whatever the reasons for failure, be honest about your achievements. Trumpet your successes by all means, but don't necessarily hide your failures. There may be lessons to be learned, experience to be disseminated, credibility to be won from explaining why the project didn't work out quite as planned.

These are the basic building ingredients of a good application. Having got this information together, you need to try and stand back a little and look at your application from a slightly different viewpoint to see if you make a good application into an even better one. The following chapter tries to shift the emphasis away from the information you need to assemble to the perspective you need to have.

Dealing with weaknesses: an example

Say you have lost money in each of the last three years. The funder may look at your accounts and think that you are slowly but surely going under and you will not be able to undertake the work you have asked them to fund. Obviously you need to reassure them that this isn't the case. How can you do this?

- **Explain why the losses came about**
  For example, are they the result of a major relocation or re-structuring (financial or staff)? If so, you can show how you have reached the end of this process and are now moving forward. Or are they the result of losing a major grant or income stream? If so, show what steps you have taken to address the short-term problem of replacing the funding (or making the necessary financial savings), and that you have put or are putting in place a new, secure and more wide-ranging income base.

- **Show how you are progressing well this year**
  Hopefully this year things are going better. Can you show that you have budgeted for a financial surplus and that you are on target to meet this? This implies that things genuinely have begun to turn around.

- **Use a business plan**
  Draw up a business plan (if you haven't done so already) which shows how you expect to make a regular surplus over the next three to five years, again pointing out the significant changes you have made and will be making to enable you to achieve this.

- **Indicate the funder's role in your development**
  It may be that you are applying to the funder specifically to help you get out of the financial mess you are in. Again, you will need to give them the confidence that you have thought through your long-term income and expenditure requirements and that you have a workable strategy in place to achieve this. Then show the funder the importance of your work and that they can be a key investor in your organisation's future growth and development.

Make a list of some of your weak points and how you might respond.

Weakness	Explanation

4 IMPROVING YOUR CHANCES

Having got together all the basic ingredients, you now need to stand back a little and bring some new thinking to bear on the applications process. This should enable you to present your work in a way that grabs the donor's attention and helps your application stand out from the crowd.

Think in project terms

The whole purpose of fundraising is getting hold of enough money to meet the day-to-day running costs for your organisation and its work and any capital expenditure that your organisation is incurring, plus the resources that you require for your future development.

But it is far easier to raise money for something specific than for the organisation as a whole. This is because donors can then match the support they give to some specific piece of work or expenditure, to a particular activity or outcome. They will feel that their money is actually doing something very specific.

So, rather than just asking for a generous contribution to your organisation or towards its overall financial needs, it is far better to ask for support for a particular aspect of your work or to pay for a specific item of expenditure.

Thinking of your work in project terms and designing projects which will attract support is a key factor of successful fundraising and proposal writing.

The ACEVO definitions

The whole core costs/project funding debate has been greatly moved on by the publication in 1999 of a report by ACEVO (Association of Chief Executives of Voluntary Organisations) entitled *Who pays for Core Costs?* and then the revision of this report in 2001 under the title of *Funding our Future*. The following is quoted from the second report, *Funding our Future*:

All organisations, whatever their mission or sector, have central costs. They need to pay for management and leadership, research and development, financial planning, management and control. These functions support the activities of the organisation, and without them the organisation cannot survive and deliver its mission. Core costs have the following features:

- *They are essential to keeping the organisation going.*
- *They tend to be needed long term, although they may fluctuate over time.*
- *They may not be attractive to donors.*

The appropriate balance between overhead and activity costs is a central preoccupation for managers in all sectors.

Voluntary organisations have a wide range of sources of income. ... The balance between these different sources of income differs from charity to charity. The 'funding mix' – and most particularly the different conditions attached to these different pieces of funding – is a central factor in the strategic management and development of voluntary organisations.

There's no such thing as core funding!

Charities often say they can get funding for projects or for capital spending but not for their administrative or core costs.

To tackle this, the first step is to eliminate these core costs as a separate item from your thinking. You do not have any costs other than those which are necessary for carrying out your work or projects. If you do you are breaking the law, because a charity can only spend money wholly and exclusively on its charitable purposes.

So, you need to:

- think of your work as a series of projects
- build your full overhead costs into each of these activities (this is now called Full Project Funding)
- recognise that if the overhead costs have not been paid for, then the project is not being fully funded.

For more information on how to do this, see Chapter 5 on Costing a Project.

The report went on to look at the 1990s funding environment, and found that:

The current funding environment is not conducive to good funding relationships.

1 *It does not allow for the creation of mature and stable voluntary organisations able to take opportunities and make a full contribution.*
2 *It does not encourage transparency, but rather the complex renaming of activities, and restructuring of organisations in pursuit of funding.*
3 *In turn this does not facilitate a creative or mature relationship between the funders and the funded.*

4 *It is extremely expensive. Voluntary organisations lose staff as projects come to an end, and then need to re-recruit; funders receive applications for activities that have just come to an end of a period of funding.*

5 *It risks public sympathy and support for voluntary organisations. At a time when donations by members of the public are seen as having reached a plateau, it is dangerous to run a funding regime that assumes the back-room costs can be met by individual donations, while front line costs are met by the statutory sector.*

This is not sensible in a climate in which the voluntary sector is expected to play an even larger role in the development and delivery of social policy.

The report went on to recognise that funders have strong reasons for preferring to support project costs only, and that voluntary organisations have adopted a range of different strategies to deal with this issue, many of which *'are inherently risky or unsustainable'.*

The report recognised two basic aspects of the problem:

- The costs of maintaining the infrastructure of individual organisations – referred to in the report as overhead costs.
- The costs of running the primary activity of the organisation.

The report suggested that it would be helpful to distinguish between these two costs, and throughout concentrated on the overhead costs. It described these costs as:

- the management costs of all activity
- the research and development capacity within voluntary organisations
- the support services – meaning the premises, IT and finance costs –as well as the administrative, personnel and training costs.

The report argued that the situation was serious enough to demand a new settlement.

There needs to be a much more mature understanding of the respective roles and responsibilities of different funders, and the ways in which they can help to meet these unavoidable costs. The current funding environment encourages management behaviours on both sides of the funding relationship that obstruct both funders and funded organisations in meeting their own objectives.

Such a new settlement will require changes both from funders and the funded. It will require voluntary organisations to:

1 *Improve internal accounting, financial management and business planning.*

2 *Develop benchmarking on overhead costs.*

3 *Innovate in order to drive down overhead costs.*

4 Demonstrate effectiveness and capacity.

5 Develop their own ways of measuring effectiveness and organisational change.

It will require funders to:

1 Meet the overhead costs associated with managing a piece of work.

2 See their funding as part of a programme of long-term investment.

3 Support the development of the management of voluntary organisations.

4 Manage change within their portfolio of grants.

5 Develop ways of evaluating effectiveness.

Crucially, the report proposed three different strategies that funders might adopt in their grant-making. 'These are alternative models of funding that seek to break the mould of the debate about core and project funding' and can be summarised as:

- **full project funding** in which all reasonable associated costs are met as part of a funding package – this is referred to as 'the business model';
- **development funding** through which the internal infrastructure costs of an organisation are met for a time in order to enable it to grow and develop;
- **strategic funding** through which the funder recognises the need for an organisation to exist – in order to meet its own objectives – and is prepared to contribute over an agreed period of time.

Some of these forms of funding will be appropriate for some types of funder, for some types of voluntary organisation, and at particular stages of a voluntary organisation's life. Funders are likely to use a combination of these strategies, and for some only one or two of the strategies will seem suitable. The report argued for:

- a more transparent approach to describing core costs
- a clear recognition that core costs are unavoidable
- a recognition that pressure needs to be exerted to keep costs low
- a recognition that there is a level below which core costs cannot reasonable fall without the funding organisation and the funded organisation incurring unacceptable risk.

The great strength of the report, apart from its clarity, was the powerful coalition behind it. The definitions are therefore becoming well-established, most notably because the *Code of Good Practice on Funding* (part of the Government's *Compact with the Voluntary Sector*) is explicit in its recognition that core costs need to be recognised by funders and it promotes the three models of funding developed in the ACEVO report.

As a result, government at all levels – in theory at least – should recognise the three funding definitions. Many major grant-making trusts do, and even the National Lottery Community Fund has now been dragged kicking and screaming into recognising the concept of full project funding.

Therefore, it is now almost always worth framing your funding application around the ACEVO definitions. You can start your applications by saying: '*I am to ask for full project funding for* ... ' or '*I am writing to ask for development funding for* ... ' or whatever. All major funders will now recognise this new code and accept that you are putting the legitimate management and other overhead costs into the project budget (for more detail see Chapter 5 on Costing a Project).

But what about getting funding for the boring bits ...?

The ACEVO report has definitely made project fundraising that much easier. However, it immediately raises the question of how you get support for those parts of your work which are less attractive to donors. There are a number of possible ways of overcoming this problem.

- **Cost all your projects realistically**. Include all the items of expenditure you are likely to incur. This is dealt with further in Chapter 5 on Costing a Project.
- **Include an allocation of overhead costs** in your project budget (full project funding). It is reasonable that every project should make an appropriate contribution to the general costs of running the organisation. This allocation should be made on some suitable basis which you are prepared to justify, rather than a figure plucked out of the air (see also Chapter 5).
- **Be creative** in how you match your income to your expenditure. Be realistic in how you cost your projects. Be imaginative in designing attractive projects to raise money for.
- **Use your core grants and general fundraising income** to pay for the administration costs or the parts of your work that it is especially difficult to raise money for.

The problem can arise that your fundraising for one particular project is so successful that you have raised more than you need or can reasonably spend on the work. What do you then do?

You must do something. If you have asked for money for a particular purpose, then you are obliged to spend it for that purpose. You will have to go back to at least some of your supporters and ask if you can use their money to extend the project or spend their grant on another related piece of work. They will almost certainly agree to this. Or you might decide to expand the project or allocate any surplus in to next year's budget; again, you should keep your supporters informed.

Difficulties arise when fundraising threatens to determine the work of the organisation. Many organisations find that it is easy to raise money for a particular purpose or decide to approach a particular line of funding which is only available for a very particular purpose, and then re-organise themselves to fit in with this. Ideally, you should first decide what you want to do and then raise money for that. There will inevitably be some trade-off between what you can easily raise money for and what you want to be doing, but you should try to keep the two in a reasonable balance. Otherwise the organisation will lose purpose and direction.

Where you judge the project to be unattractive for fundraising, you will need to think carefully. It will be a waste of your time to seek funds for something that is unlikely to appeal to donors. In such circumstances, you might:

- find a way of restructuring the project, or presenting it in a different way so that it appears more attractive to donors;
- think of something else to raise money for, which will be more attractive. Most organisations can juggle their budgets so that the more attractive projects are put forward for fundraising and the remainder of the money comes through the general fundraising income it is receiving;
- discuss whether there are alternative ways of financing the project (for example through charging fees for services or developing a new income stream). Many people tend to be rather grants obsessed. Always ask yourself whether short-term grants are the only way or the best way of resourcing the project.

A fundable project should be:

- **specific** – an identifiable item of expenditure or aspect of the organisation's work
- **important** – both to the organisation and to the cause or need it is meeting. If there is some long-term impact, that will be an added bonus
- **effective** – there should be a clear and positive outcome
- **realistic** – the work proposed should be achievable
- **good value** – the work should be a good use of the donor's money
- **topical** – it should be looking at current issues and concerns
- **relevant** – it should be relevant to the donor and the donor's particular funding concerns
- **bite-sized** – it should not be too large or too small for a donor to support, although the cost might be shared through several smaller grants. If it is too large, it might be broken down further into sub-projects.

Making a project more fundable

Once you have decided that you are going to raise money for a project, the next step is to see whether and how you can make it more attractive to donors. Donors will certainly want to see value for their money, and possibly some long-term impact on the organisation they are investing in. This improvement process will also allow you to think through what you are doing, and even help you create a better project – which is an added benefit.

Exercise

Go round the organisation and get a list of 20 things that colleagues want funded. Rank them in terms of fundability. Do they form the basis of a good fundraising programme?

Grant-winning ideas and fundable projects

What is a good idea? A good idea is something that will have immediate appeal with donors as being different, lively, worthwhile and worth funding. The donor's first response is more likely to be *'Gosh, that sounds good; we ought to be backing that'*, rather than, *'I've had ten applications like that in the last month, and none of them are likely to achieve very much'*.

Good ideas are central to good fundraising. Even the very best application may not make up for a poorly thought-out project or for something that simply is not very interesting. However, it is difficult to define what constitutes a good idea. Usually it is something that leaps out at you from the page, and seems obvious once someone has thought of it. The following are some ingredients of a good idea.

- It meets a **really important and urgent need**.
- It is **fresh or interesting** (or at least sounds it) and captures the imagination.
- It is – or sounds – **startlingly obvious**, even though nobody has thought of it before.
- It has a **catchy title**.
- It is or appears **innovative**.
- It is **topical** – it fits within current fashions, thinking, concerns.
- It addresses issues of **disadvantage**, a key concern for most funders.
- It is **different** – it stands out in the crowd of more ordinary applications.
- It has **different aspects** which appeal to different funding constituencies (wide appeal).
- It shows **value for money** or **leverage** (a small input with lots and lots of output).

- It **complements and supplements existing provision** or involves collaboration with other agencies.
- It has **a clear and attainable objective**.
- It has **measurable benefits** and specific outputs.
- It is **realistic** and **achievable**.
- It is **fundable**, and may even **develop its own income** in the long term.

How to develop good ideas

Respond to new needs as they emerge. You are at the front line of social provision. The needs you identify today will be met by the established services of tomorrow.

Two heads are better than one. Get together with colleagues to bounce ideas around. Or just wallow in a warm bath!

Start with your current work, your current projects. What are the next steps? How could things be done differently or better? What new needs are emerging from what you are doing and what can you do about them?

Ask your current, previous and potential users. What do they think about the situation now and in the future? What would they do in your position?

Also, keep an eye on the 'marketplace' – see what others are doing. Get hold of other organisations' annual reports. Look at the emerging social business sector. Keep in touch with social trends, emerging fashions and fads.

Write down ideas as soon as you have thought of them, however half-baked or ill thought-out they appear. If you don't, you'll forget them. If you do, you can develop and refine them over time.

Bring in outsiders who have no preconceptions. This can provide a degree of 'lateral thinking' which will be useful. You know how the buses or the health service should be run, so it is a good bet that outsiders can teach you a thing or two. Stop thinking about what you can't do and about 'all the problems and difficulties'. Develop a positive can-do attitude to your work and your organisation.

Go back to basics. Forget what you are doing now. What might you be doing in an ideal world to deal with the problem or need? Look at your organisation's objects or purposes as enshrined in the founding documents and think about what you would do if you were starting from scratch.

Somewhere, there is an idea which is just right for your organisation, which will be easy to raise money for, which will enhance your credibility and public image, and which (hopefully) will solve all your financial problems … for ever!

Adding value

Wherever possible, try to show the funder that you are giving and getting maximum value from their support. Investment, leverage, dissemination and evaluation are all useful concepts in this process

1 Investment

An investment (or 'development' expenditure in ACEVO terms) is an expenditure which builds the potential of the organisation and helps it move towards a more successful future. It aims to build a more secure and successful organisation later on rather than simply provide a service now. It can be an extremely important and cost-effective way of providing support. Some possibilities are listed below.

- **Investing in capacity**: to enable you to undertake more work more effectively or to earn more money from the services you provide.
- **Investing in technology**: to open up new, quicker, lower cost ways of providing services, or to help you move from being a local to a national or international information provider.
- **Investing in efficiency**: to streamline the organisation and cut waste.
- **Investing in training and skills**: to improve the quality and effectiveness of your work.
- **Investing in plant or equipment**: for example, buying a piece of equipment to improve your efficiency or effectiveness.
- **Investing in fundraising**: for example, developing a supporter group which over time will generate an increased income.
- **Investing in long-term stability**: for example, generating the resources or information which will enable you to negotiate contracts and service agreements which will underpin your future financial security.

All these can be the subject of a fundraising application. Indeed, you can often put on a gloss which makes the idea appear more planned and thought out than it in fact was. If you realise that you are currently short of money and have ideas for future income generation, you could dress this up as a stage one/stage two proposal. This is where you show how you have reached the end of the first stage of your development and you need to get to the next stage; you ask for funding to help you get from where you are to where you need to be.

2 Leverage

Leverage is the process whereby a small amount of support helps create a large amount of impact. This is the ideal position for a donor, so showing leverage can improve your chances of success. There are many ways in which this can be done.

- **Matching grants**: where one donor has promised to pay half the costs if you can raise the rest. Every pound you now raise will release an additional pound of the donor's money. This is often used by companies when they match their employees' fundraising activities pound for pound.
- **Challenge grants**: where you ask a donor to promise a certain sum of money on the condition that you raise the rest by a certain date. This gives the donor the assurance that their promise of money is being used to lever other sums, and the confidence that if you fail to raise the outstanding amounts the original donor owes nothing.
- **Fundraising leverage**: where the support given will enable you to raise a much larger sum. A prize offered for a raffle, for example, may enable you to raise a considerable sum through selling raffle tickets. Or integrated software would allow you to develop a membership and alumni programme worth X hundred thousand pounds a year.
- **Lasting benefit**: your work can have a long-term benefit in the lives of individuals and their communities, and this can last way beyond the time you are supporting them.
- **Use of volunteers**: the value of the work done could be much greater if volunteers rather than paid staff are used.
- **Discounts**: obtaining discounts on purchases or even getting items on your budget donated free shows an effective organisation and allows the donor's contribution to go that much further.
- **Problem solving**: by meeting the need now you then save money which would otherwise have to be spent dealing with the consequences (for example if you stop young people turning to crime).

3 Dissemination

People will be interested in the impact of your work, and its effect on alleviating the problem. If the money is to undertake research or produce a publication, they will want to be told how the research findings will be disseminated or how the publication will be distributed. If the money is for some form of innovation or a pilot project, they will want to be shown how the success of the project will be measured, and what will be done subsequently to promote the lessons learned and encourage others to replicate the ideas.

Dissemination can be linked to the concept of leverage. For example, a locally run project can be copied throughout the country if it can be shown to be effective, so X thousand pounds given to you to test out the idea means that ultimately the whole country might benefit.

The application for funds is just the first part of the process. Obtaining the money and undertaking the work outlined in the proposal is the second stage. The third stage is to make use of the outcome in some way – and where this is an important ingredient of the proposal, it should be fully discussed in the application.

4 Evaluation

Increasingly funders require the organisations they support to produce some sort of evaluation of the outcome of their work. This means setting measurable objectives for your project and then measuring the results you achieve – whether this is the number of people attending your activities or changes in attitude or behaviour towards the problem. Evaluation is particularly important for the National Lottery Community Fund.

Many applications are disappointingly vague about what they will actually do and how they will measure progress. The key thing is firstly to set some measurable targets, and secondly to show how discussions about progress will be fed into the management of the project (and, indeed, the management of the organisation). There is little point saying: *'We are behind (or ahead) of our targets'* and then do nothing about it. Monitoring and evaluation is about action and decision-making. You need to show who will take action and when.

This will not only demonstrate how effective you are – and if you can do this you will find it that much easier to obtain funding in the future – but it will also provide you with a tool to manage your project, to make the appropriate changes and adjustments as the work proceeds.

Evaluation can cost a good deal of money (for example, for professional consultancy, surveys and other market research, or the work involved in the measurement of outcomes). From time to time, it may be appropriate for an organisation to undertake a serious evaluation with the aim of setting the stage for its future development. Indeed the costs of this can be packaged up into a 'project' and be the subject of a fundraising application. But evaluation need not cost much if it is thought through and built into the way the project is run right from the start. Evaluation of what you do shows a professional approach, and in a competitive world, this can only be an advantage.

Chapters 2 and 3 have looked at what you need to put into an application and how you can give it the fundraising edge. Having decided on what you want to apply for, the next thing to look at is how to make sure you are asking for the right amount of money.

5 COSTING A PROJECT

The budget

The budget is a central element of your application. It sets out your financial need and provides the base around which your argument for support is developed.

People are often frightened by the budgeting process. They give it an aura and mystique that it simply does not have, and wrongly assume that it is a skill possessed only by the privileged few. Budgeting is no more than a careful costing of all the items of expenditure involved in the work you are proposing. But since many of the items cannot be precisely determined or allocated, there is plenty of scope for creativity in coming to a final figure for your fundraising.

A common mistake is for people to under-cost their budgets. Perhaps they feel that if they apply for less, they stand a better chance of getting the money. But if you always apply for too little, you will end up in a financial mess.

It is better to go for a larger sum when raising money, particularly where the project is well thought through and likely to be attractive to donors. You will then be concentrating your effort on the fundraising which is most likely to succeed. By including overhead costs and allowing for other costs which you might have otherwise omitted, you will be bringing money into your organisation which you would otherwise have to raise in other ways.

The trick is to demonstrate the benefits of the project and how much will be achieved by the work – rather than showing how little it will cost to do it. Remember, fundraising is about change rather than money. Sell the idea of change, and then tell the donor how much it will cost.

The budgeting process

There are basically six stages in the budgeting process. Here are two examples of different kinds of projects, one mainly capital, the second mainly revenue. They follow through the same six stages.

Stages in the budgeting process

1 Describe the project
2 Write down the expenditure needs
3 Cost each item as carefully as you can
4 Add up all the costs
5 Examine the total and amend the budget if necessary
6 Agree the budget

Example 1 – Upgrading a community centre

Stage 1

Describe in detail the scope of the project and what you intend to do with the money. Compare the following statements:

- we plan to refurbish our community centre;
- we plan to develop our community centre by creating new community initiatives and increasing capacity.

These are two very different fundraising propositions. The first is internally focused and centres on maintenance. The second is about using a building to advance the organisation and its work. It involves additional costs and will be more expensive, but it is also likely to be more attractive to donors. In ACEVO terms it would be called a 'development grant' (see Chapter 4).

This applies to any kind of capital or equipment purchase. *'We want to buy a building'* or *'We need a minibus'* are pretty dull statements. *'We want to release the creative talents of our young people by setting up a community arts centre'*, or *'We want to overcome the problems of rural isolation by bringing older people together twice a week'* are much more engaging. It's not about your needs, it's about your users' needs. Talk about them, not you.

Stage 2

Write down a list of all the budget heads of expenditure. Then think if you have left anything out. Refurbishing the community centre could include:

- feasibility studies
- architect
- quantity surveyor/structural engineer (if there is major building work)
- health and safety advice
- construction costs
- furniture and fittings
- security (system and people)
- decoration

- equipment
- maintenance
- sundry and contingency costs

Stage 3

Cost each item using the best estimates you can.

- **Professional fees** (for example architect): get different quotes and see what is included in each. Can you get drawings and plans done for free on a joint risk venture (i.e. if you get the money they get the architect's contract, but if you don't raise the money you don't owe the architect anything)?
- **Furniture and fittings**: you may be able to get some of these items donated (for example paint, chairs and settees) or at least at a discount. If so, quote prices before discount and treat any discount as in-kind support as part of your fundraising.
- **Security**: this can include people as well as equipment. For example, if you are open in the evening you may well need extra security such as CCTV and additional reception cover. You need to take account of any increased running costs in your budget for running the centre.
- **Maintenance**: buildings get bashed about; there is wear and tear on equipment. Broken equipment will need to be replaced and the place kept in good order. You may even need to appoint a warden or caretaker for the first time. All these are extra running costs which you will need to take into account.

Stage 4

Add up the estimated costs to create a total budget for the project. Some of these costs will be one-off (such as construction costs); others will be on-going (such as repair, maintenance and caretaking).

The one-off costs tend to be fairly straightforward, but make sure you get more than one quote. The on-going costs can be more problematic as the budget for refurbishment will not usually cover these. But you could think of including additional first year running costs in your fundraising budget, just to help you get going in your new premises. Do add in lost income for the time the existing centre will be closed for refurbishment. The basic rule is decide what you think is reasonable and, at this stage, put down your best estimate of the cost.

Stage 5

Examine the total to decide whether it provides a reasonable basis for your fundraising. Is the end figure you have arrived at too high, too low or about right? This decision is more likely to be based on the overall costs set against the benefits you will be aiming to deliver for your community. For example, £100,000 for a thriving centre which will be used by 750 people a week is not much money at all; £30,000 so that a couple of small youth groups can meet on a Wednesday and Thursday evening sounds a lot. Further, if you can show that once all this work is done you will the have a sustainable income base from the hire out charges you will be able to levy, this makes it doubly attractive to a funder. Attach a three-year plan to demonstrate all of this.

It is usually possible to re-cost the project so that the total comes out significantly higher or lower. Many of the items are simply best guesses at this stage, and only time will tell.

Once you are confident that your estimated costs are all plausible – that is, you can defend them when they are put under the spotlight by a sceptical grants assessor – and that the project represents real value for money, the final question is whether the total required is too much for one particular donor to support. If so, approach several donors. You can even break down the project into bite-sized chunks, asking one donor to support the children's play room, another the computers for the homework club and IT centre, etc.

Stage 6

You now have a final, agreed budget for your project. This is the target for your fundraising, and the basis on which you can create a fundraising plan.

Example 2 – An outreach project

Often it is not simply a question of calculating the direct costs of a project. Sometimes you will want to include an allocation of overheads or a contribution to your organisation's central administration costs, especially when applying for salaries and other revenue funding. This is now called 'full project funding' (*see page 35*) and is a perfectly reasonable thing to do.

The basis on which these costs are apportioned will vary from project to project, but it should be based on a sensible apportionment of the costs. The budgeting is the same six-stage process. To avoid repetition, we are only expanding on points which are particularly relevant to revenue applications – otherwise the points made in the previous example above are all valid.

Stage 1 – Describe the project

We wish to help people out of poverty and to take more control over their lives by helping them achieve greater financial independence. We will do this by establishing a new money advice service.

Stage 2 – Write down the expenditure

- Salary/National Insurance for the money advice worker
- Basic equipment needs (new desk, computer, etc.)
- Premises costs (rent, rates, heat, light, cleaning, etc.)
- Post, telephone, stationery, etc.
- Central costs (insurance, bank charges, accountancy, audit, etc.)
- Management/supervision costs
- Volunteer expenses
- Clerical support
- Travel

> There's no such thing as 'core costs'! All your costs are spent on the work you do. Therefore, make sure you build all relevant overhead costs into each 'project' application you make, and call it 'full project funding'.

Charities often say that they can get funding for project or for capital spending, but not for their administrative or core costs. Core costs typically include:

- general management salaries
- administration salaries
- rent, rates, heat, light and other property costs
- telephone, stationery and photocopying
- accountancy and audit
- insurance
- legal costs

The key to overcoming this is to eliminate these core costs as a separate item in your thinking. You do not have any core costs. The only costs you carry are those which are necessary for undertaking your work, unless you have people who are doing absolutely nothing. Therefore, you need to build these overhead costs into all your activities and recognise that unless they have been funded insufficient money has been raised for the project.

Putting down all the direct costs is usually a fairly straightforward process. The difficult part can be remembering all those hidden costs which are vital to the project's success but which are far less obvious (for example occupancy of the building, management and administration costs). However, make sure you get all of them down.

Stage 3 – Cost each item

Again, the direct costs are fairly easy to put a figure on. You know the expected salary of the worker. You know what kind of basic equipment he or she will need. However, how do you calculate the central costs?

The most common way of calculating central costs is to look at the percentage of space the person will take up and of the office facilities he or she will share. For example, if the outreach worker will use one fifth of the office building, allocate one fifth of the premises costs (rent, rates, heat, light, etc.) to the project. If the outreach worker shares office facilities equally with eight other full-time workers, allocate one eighth of the post, telephone, stationery and other such bills. If the outreach project occupies a quarter of the manager's time in terms of development, support and supervision, allocate a quarter of the manager's salary and national insurance to the project.

Make a reasonable estimate. In the end, all you are trying to achieve is a realistic figure for the cost to the organisation as a whole of running this new project. It is not a fiddle. You are not trying quietly to bump up the figures and apply for more than you should. Rather, you are simply aiming to avoid the position whereby you suddenly find the telephone bill has risen substantially on account of this new project and this becomes a drain on your resources.

Stage 4 – Total the costs

Total the costs up on the above basis. Make sure that you explain how you have arrived at the costs in notes to your budget, as follows:

Salary & National Insurance	£16,500
Premises costs [1]	£8,200
Supervision and support [2]	£7,500
Volunteer expenses [3]	£6,000
Other	£6,800
TOTAL	£45,000

Notes
[1] equal to 20% of occupancy costs
[2] equal to 25% of management and 12.5% of admin salaries
[3] calculated on the basis of 6 full time equivalent volunteers at £750 per annum travel costs and £250 training costs

Stage 5

When looking at the overall costs, again you can change them if you are not happy with them. Re-assess the resources required and adjust the percentages you have used accordingly. Remember you may be asked to justify the basis of your calculation, so it has to appear reasonable.

If you already have a grant which covers some or all of your central costs (say from your local authority), you can use this to show that you have already covered some of the costs of the project. Therefore, if you can show that you have already raised £15,700 you have already covered your premises and supervision costs from another grant. It is important that you do this for four reasons:

(i) It demonstrates to the funder that you have not forgotten anything. If you simply leave these costs out because they have already been paid for, then the funder may get the impression that you haven't thought the project through properly.

(ii) The hardest part of your fundraising is getting the fundraising ball rolling. Once you have started getting money in, other funders take confidence from this and pledge their support accordingly. So if you can show that some of the required money is already there, this gives the whole thing an impetus that it otherwise would not have.

(iii) It shows that you have a really good grasp of finance, knowing what parts of your work are already covered by existing grants and income, and which are not.

(iv) It creates extra leverage to your application because the new funder only has to give two-thirds of the total to make this wonderful work happen.

Stage 6 – Agree the budget

As with the example of the community centre above, you should now be clear where the money for the different parts of the organisation's costs are coming from, as well as having an agreed fundraising plan. Project fundraising can feel a bit like being a juggler and keeping lots of different fundraising balls in the air at the same time. The advantage is that if you can do it, you broaden your fundraising scope and become less dependent on one major funder.

Common mistakes in budgeting

Forgotten costs

Have you included *all* the items you will be spending money on? What about training and attending courses? Buying necessary publications? Travel and subsistence? Pensions as well as National Insurance? Who is going to pay for these if you don't raise the money? Or will this extra expenditure just increase your deficit?

Hidden costs

Every project consumes office space, heating, lighting, telephone, postage, the cost of supervision by the director and the committee of management. You need to include a reasonable element of them in your budget for the project.

Since it is far easier to raise money for projects than it is for administration or running the office, by allocating your overhead costs onto your projects, you will use the glamour of the project to get the unattractive administrative costs paid for.

Understated costs

It is easy to put too low a cost in your budget. There are several reasons for this. There is a tendency to underestimate the costs of the project because you think that the fundraising will be difficult. Or you may be basing your estimate on this year's costs, or worse, on last year's, but your budget is for next year when inflation will have increased the cost of everything. Get as good an estimate as possible for the cost of each item and allow something for inflation.

When you are applying for a grant over several years, allow for inflation on an estimated basis for the second and subsequent years (you would normally state the assumptions you have made in a footnote to the budget).

If you leave out any item of expenditure from your budget or put in a cost which is less than what will actually be incurred, then you will be out of pocket. If you consistently do this, then you will have a financial problem. It also looks extremely bad from a fundraising point of view if you have to go back to a funder asking for more money simply because you under-estimated the costs.

Doing what you say you will do

If you say that you *will* do something, and you take money on that basis, then you *must* spend the money in the way you have proposed. If you can't, then you will have to discuss the situation with the donor, or return the money. Therefore, don't promise what you cannot deliver simply because it would make the proposal more attractive to the funder.

Some donors may require you to spend the grant precisely as you have indicated in your budget, and require audited accounts demonstrating that you have done just this. Other donors are happy so long as you have spent the money roughly as detailed in the budget for the purposes set out in the application (they do not care if you have spent more on some items, less on others; they are more interested in the fact that the work you have proposed has actually been done).

Funding regimes are generally getting tighter rather than looser. If you have any concerns about the terms of a grant, or are expecting that there may be changes for whatever good reason, contact the donor sooner rather than later and explain the situation. Donors appreciate openness and are generally happy to be flexible in these kind of circumstances. However, they get very sniffy if they think you have tried to go behind their backs or have misapplied money. In any case, your auditor will want to examine the basis on which the grants were received, and how the money was spent. You may want to check with the donor at the time you accept the grant what reporting arrangements (if any) will be required.

6 IMPROVING YOUR COMMUNICATION SKILLS

Writing in plain English

Faced with the task of writing an application, some people find it hard to put their thoughts together in a clear, logical way. Others develop a writer's block, so that although they have thought through what they want to say, they don't actually get round to putting anything in writing.

An application is no more than answering simple questions such as:

- Who are you?
- What do you currently do?
- What do you want to do?
- Why is this work important?
- What do you need to enable you to do it?
- How can the donor help you?

If you were answering these questions in conversation, you would become really enthusiastic. And in doing so, you would then enthuse the person you were approaching for money.

In your written application, you have to try to create this same sense of up-beat enthusiasm as you would in conversation. Picture yourself chatting at a bar or over coffee, trying to persuade someone of the importance of what you are doing and why they should give their support. That is what your written application is all about.

Other points to bear in mind.

1 You should put down your thoughts in an ordered way, and be as clear and succinct as you can.
2 You should make every word work for you as you have limited space, and the attention span of the reader will be short.

3 Your application is being read along with hundreds of others each month. It should be clearly set out and easy to read.

A well-written application can make the difference

A well-written application will certainly improve your chances. You will not only have marshalled your ideas and the argument for supporting you in a more persuasive and readable way, but you will also have given the reader the impression that you are well-organised and capable; sufficiently so to be entrusted with their money as the following (true) story shows.

A friend (whom we shall call Paul) was raising money for a conference in Manchester in which homeless people would speak out about homelessness issues. He was jointly organising this with someone (Peter) who worked for a homelessness charity. They agreed that they would approach a major company based in the area.

Peter organised a meeting with the company without telling Paul, who was putting together a written application. Peter rang Paul after the meeting to say not to bother putting an application in as the company wasn't interested. Paul said it was too late as he had already posted it. Paul got a phone call the next day to say that the company was giving £1,500 to the conference. This was based purely on the fact that the application accurately reflected both a really exciting project and an understanding of the company's desire to be seen as a good corporate citizen.

Some common writer's diseases

Verbicide

Using words whose meaning has been killed. Avoid using jargon – the words that only you and the professionals in your field know the meaning of. In an application you are usually talking to people who know little of the detail of what you are doing, and are unlikely to understand the specialist words which you take for granted.

'We believe that children, given the right environment, have an enormous, but often untapped, potential to learn. The concept of the learning organisation/company, in many ways, has now become commonplace. We believe that this concept, replicated in communities, could have significant benefits.'

What is a 'learning organisation' or 'learning company'? Although this is central to the application it is never explained. Therefore, unless the funder is an authority on educational issues they will not understand what the project is really about.

'Short-term respite care and flexible day care are the two most valuable forms of support for sufferers of Alzheimer's disease which allows the carer to cope longer in the community.'

What on earth does this mean? What is flexible day care and short term respite care? And why are they valuable? You may know the answers. Your readers (unless they are specialists in the caring business) are unlikely to.

Verbitis

Using inflamed words, such as unsubstantiated superlatives. Words and phrases such as 'desperate', 'unique', 'a major new initiative' have lost their meaning through over-use and should be avoided if possible. The reader will also be reading dozens of other applications all of which show desperate needs and unique solutions to the urgent problem. They want to know the facts and the figures, not the generalities expressed in the same meaningless superlatives.

Also, avoid the 'everybody knows' syndrome, where you make a bland statement on the assumption that the reader will understand its full significance. *'We all know that crime in general and youth crime in particular is on the increase. We also know that government initiatives to tackle these problems have failed.'* Do we? In any case this doesn't convince the reader that you are particularly on top of your subject. If you can't show a deep understanding of the issues, how can you persuade the reader that you have a clearly workable solution.

'Our college is a unique institution in British higher education... Our facilities are woefully inadequate... We operate in a very desolate and most deprived area.'

Be positive – 1

So many applications are couched in 'hopes' and 'maybes'. Be upbeat.

Don't say 'This project aims to'; say 'We will'.

Don't say 'It is our hope that'; say 'We expect to'.

Don't say 'If this project didn't happen then'; say 'This project will'.

Be positive – 2

So many applications are full of false gloom

Don't say 'If nothing is done the situation will just get worse and worse';

say: 'We can work to ensure that things get much better'.

This comes from a major university appeal in London. It raises more questions than answers. Be specific. Explain exactly what you mean. Why is the institution unique? Why are the facilities inadequate? Why is the area desolate? How deprived is it?

Verbosity

Just waffling on and on and on. You drown the meaning in a sea of useless words. Make every word work for you. Use a red pen to strike out what is meaningless, what adds nothing to your case. If there is very little left after doing this, then this gives you the opportunity to make a better case.

'Within our play centre, staff are required to enable us to register with Social Services and therefore operate within the law. A particularly high level of skill and understanding are needed in this sensitive area and therefore we feel it particularly useful to have the continuity of qualified staff to maintain the high level of confidence needed in the provision of this service, that is so vital to maintain free access to the centre.'

This paragraph is elaborating on the need for paid staff to run a play centre within a community education facility. Apart from the points that paid staff for the play centre are a requirement and that operating a play centre is essential to provide access to the facilities of the centre, how much of the rest of this paragraph is necessary?

There are two further and extremely common means of padding out applications.

- Many organisations describe their structure along these lines: *'XXX is a registered charity and a voluntary organisation'*. This is normally redundant information. It will be obvious from the nature of your work and your letterhead what your legal status is. A donor will only want to know if you are not a charity, as this can affect how the grant is paid over.
- Towards the end of the application, many people sign off with long-winded pleasantries, such as: *'I hope you will be able to give favourable consideration to our request for support and if you would like to discuss this initiative further or require more information, please do not hesitate to contact me at the above address.'*

> Make yourselves sound more active and dynamic by using the active rather than passive voice
>
> 'We helped Beth to ...' rather than 'Beth was helped by our organisation to ...'
>
> 'We work closely with ...' rather than 'A partnership was formed between us and ...'

Verbification

Producing a continuous stream of syllables where it could expressed more succinctly simply by tightening up your language.

- Avoid **longer words**, where shorter words will do:
  Not *personal motorised transportation*, but *private car*
  Not the *anticipated cost of the project*, but the *budget for the project*

- Avoid **long sentences**. Use punctuation to make the meaning clearer
- Avoid **long paragraphs**, which can become unreadable
- Aim for a **tabloid** rather than a broadsheet style.

> **'There's no way I talk in clichés.'**
> So avoid them like the plague!

Some practical next steps

- **Buy yourself a red pen**. Use it to shorten and tighten up the next application you write, a highlighter to note the points that are unclear, badly explained or where more information is needed, and a pencil to make marginal notes.
- **Find yourself a journalist** – possibly on your local newspaper. They are used to writing for popular consumption and fitting what they want to say into a limited space. Perhaps they can offer you valuable tips and advice on your writing style.
- **Find yourself a fundraising buddy**. Find someone else who is writing fundraising applications. Agree to read and comment on their applications if they do the same for yours. They should know little or nothing about your work, because most donors are in the same position. Ask them to tell you which bits they don't understand, what you have left out and whether they think you have made a good case.

Exercise

Rewrite the following sentences:

- It would be our hope that you might fund this project.

- A demonstrated commitment to co-operation and collaboration forms the cornerstone of this partnership.

- This book was written on the understanding that it would provide ...

- We can assure you that any contribution you would be able to make would be used to ...

- Your grant has proved to be of great significance to this organisation, and we would like to express our gratitude.

Or look at the following supplied by the *Plain English Campaign:*

What on earth do these sentences mean?

1 'Making a skill adjustment.'

2 'Achieving a positive budget variance.'

3 'Meaningful down turn in aggregate output.'

4 'Grain-consuming animal units.'

5 'An unselected roll-back to idle.'

6 'Localised capacity deficiencies.'

7 'High-quality learning environments are a necessary pre-condition for facilitation and enhancement of the on-going learning process.'

8 'If there are any points on which you require explanation or further particulars we shall be glad to furnish such additional details as may be required by telephone.'

9 'A device or arrangement that may be used to permit a patient to lie down when the need to do so is a consequence of the patient's condition rather than a need for active examination, diagnostic investigation, manipulative treatment, obstetric delivery or transport.'

10 'Any resolution which, if carried, would, in the opinion of the chairman, substantially increase the expenditure upon any service which is under the management of or reduce the revenue at the disposal of any committee, or which would involve capital expenditure, shall, when proposed and seconded, stand adjourned without discussion to the next ordinary meeting of the council, and any committee affected by it shall consider whether it desires to report thereon.'

Answers

1 Making a lot of staff redundant.
2 Making a lot of staff redundant.
3 A recession.
4 Farm animals such as cows, pigs or sheep.
5 The plane's engine failed in mid-flight.
6 Traffic bottlenecks.

7 Children need good schools.
8 Please ring if you have any questions.
9 A bed.
10 The council's committees have no power over financial matters.

Exercise

The cardinal sins of proposal writing are:

1 verbicide
2 verbitis
3 verbosity
4 verbification

Take a fundraising application you or a colleague have previously written, and rewrite it avoiding the four Vs. Aim to cut its length by at least 25%.

Tips for better writing

Do

- write in **shorter sentences**
- **break up longer sentences** into a number of sentences
- use **bullet points** to break up long sections of text.
- **vary the length** of sentences to avoid monotony
- use **shorter rather than longer words**. Say '*about*' rather than '*approximately*'; '*try*' rather than '*endeavour*'; '*often*' rather than '*frequently*')
- use **facts rather than opinions**
- keep it **short and simple**, but make sure you say all you need
- make it **clear and logical**
- keep **cross references to a minimum**. Otherwise it can all get too confusing
- improve the **visual appearance** and readability by using shorter paragraphs, headings and sub-heads, indented tables and bullet points rather than continuous prose
- **write for the reader**, with an understanding of their level of knowledge and their perception of the problem

Eh?

Pseuds Corner in *Private Eye* usually provides an object lesson in how not to write. For example:

'The folk/fairytale Cinderella has a four thousand year old history and indicates a paradigm that predates the rise of the fairytale and psychoanalysis. Patterns of a hypnogogic flow or destructuring and a hypnopompic flow or restructuring indicate the capacity to symbolise. Some aspects of projective identification act as a defence whereas anticipatory identification permits a prospective element. Symbol formation contains both regressive and progresive components which are essential for learning and growth.'

Don't

- use **jargon**. Only use words that you can guarantee your reader will understand

- make **bland assertions** – *'extremely busy'*, *'well-attended'*, *'massive increase'* – give figures

- use **unsubstantiated superlatives** – *'desperate need'*, *'absolutely unique'*, *'tragic waste of glorious human potential'* etc.

- **assume knowledge** – 'You will, I am sure, be familiar with the problems of ...' Will they?

- **patronise** either the donor or the beneficiaries.

- use words or concepts which will be **controversial or inflammatory**. Talk in a common language and build bridges from where you are to where they are

- use **three words when one will do**. Rather than saying *'From the evidence we have collected it appears that ...'* say *'Research shows that ...'*; don't say *'In the region of ...'* say *'About ...'*

- use **redundant information** e.g. *'XXX is a registered charity and a voluntary organisation.'* It will be on your letterhead.

- **shift fundraising responsibility** – *'if you could support our appeal or know of any other company which might'* – have your own clear fundraising plan

---

Sentence length

Long sentences can be a real problem for readers because when the end eventually arrives, and it can be a long time in coming, they may have forgotten the beginning, especially when it contains many different ideas or many branches of a main idea, and even if they haven't they will have lost interest well before you get to the full stop. And if there's another long sentence straight after there is a clear danger that they will give up totally because they just can't be bothered with the major mental effort you are requiring of them.

But short sentences can get on your nerves. Especially one after another. There's no variety. It's too abrupt. No flow. A real pain.

So vary the length of your sentences to achieve a nice balance. The average sentence length over the document should be around 15 words.

Using different media

You can produce your application in whatever form you want. However, be aware of the following.

- **Hand-written letters**: generally only do this if it is a short covering letter to someone you know. Even then, make sure it is neat and in black ink. Assume it is going to be photocopied.

- **Typed**: you want the letter to appear personalised. This doesn't mean the content has to be different in every letter you write. However, each letter should have the person's name and address typed on it and you should usually hand write *'Dear …'* and sign the letter yourself with your name typed underneath. (Obviously it is different if you are writing to 10,000 members.)

- **Print quality**: try to ensure that the letter looks well-produced.

- **Fax/e-mail**: a few donors are happy to receive applications this way. Most aren't. Only do this if the guide books or the donors themselves suggest this as an option.

- **Cassettes/videos**: these are usually best offered rather than sent. Few funders are so committed to their work that they want to listen to your appeal on the way home or watch it in the evening. If they are, they can always contact you for a copy. Also, they cannot photocopy tapes and videos to circulate to their trustees.

  The point at which videos especially come into their own is when you are making a presentation to a company for a major sponsorship, or to an audience of potential donors. If you are speaking to donors, you will need back-up literature for people to take away or pledge forms to be signed there and then.

- **Telephone**: telephone sales techniques applied to appeals are being used more and more, especially if there is an obvious case for telephoning. This could work for alumni, membership and other constituency appeals where people expect to be asked to give, or if there is an extremely urgent reason to give now (for example disaster appeals).

  The telephone can also be used to follow up a written approach. A major disability charity was hosting a prestigious gala dinner at which it wished to sell tables to company executives. The organiser rang her target list of companies, explained what was going on and asked if she could fax details there and then. She rang back a short time later to see what more information the company needed, but most just agreed there and then. All the tables were booked up within two days. However, cold-calling grant-making trusts is not a good idea. They want written applications.

- **Website**: you can direct donors to your website if they need more information about your organisation and its work. But make sure that the design and content of your website are good enough.

7 BEFORE YOU WRITE

Donor research

Before you write an application, you need to know who you are writing to and what they are interested in. The perfect application to the wrong person will not get the money. An application is a communication from you (*who needs the money*) to the donor (*who has the money*). It will only be effective as a communication if it recognises their particular interests and concerns.

So the first thing to do is to find out as much as possible about the donor. Information is relatively easy to come by – from grants guides, from literature produced by the funding sources (most of the larger trusts and the major companies publish reports or produce information for applicants; read this carefully and read between the lines too), from personal contact at meetings and conferences, from gossip 'on the grapevine'. If there's a specific question you need answering, you can always telephone. So try to find out the following:

- **Who** is the person who will be dealing with your application? This is the 'Correspondent', who you will be writing to. Their job is to progress the application through the decision-making system, seeking professional or technical advice if necessary – and they may reject the application immediately as being of little relevance or interest to them. Make sure you have their name and job title correct, and that you understand their interests and values. Avoid the application looking like a circular at all costs. Applications which look like circulars, however well designed, are almost always rejected straight away.
- Is there an **application form**? Some funders, such as the Lottery distribution boards and BBC Children in Need, require you to fill in an application form. In terms of the kind of things you will write and the issues you will deal with the same general principles apply for an application form and when you write a letter. Ring up beforehand if you are not sure if they have an application form.

- **Which budget** is the money coming from? This particularly applies to companies. If you are asking for a donation, this will come from the donations budget and you will need to write to the manager of the charitable donations. If you are proposing a formal sponsorship, this may come from the marketing budget, so you will be writing to the head of marketing. This can also apply to other funders. Some trusts, for example, fund UK-wide but have preferences for certain local areas and allocate some of their annual budget accordingly. If you operate in one of these local areas, stress the importance of your project to local people and show how it is integrated into the local community. Avoid the impression that you are really a national or regional project which happens to be based in that local area.

- What can you learn from **policies, priorities and guidelines for applicants**? What are they really interested in supporting? Are there particular exclusions, types of project or expenditure which the donor will not support in any circumstances? Many of the larger donors now have websites with up-to-date policy details.

- **What grants** have they made previously, and for what sorts of purposes? Can you learn anything from this? For example, do they favour classical arts or community arts? Do they give a higher priority to promoting artistic excellence or involving new people in arts activities? Do they want to bring new audiences to the arts and, if so, do they require you to offer full disabled access at your premises?

- **Are they conventional or radical** in approach? Do they appear to play safe or to take risks? Do they support campaigns? Does any of this have implications for the way in which you describe yourselves? For example, grant-making trusts are often seen as the risk takers, the ones who will push back the boundaries of current provision by funding emerging needs and new approaches to old needs. Very few of them, however, report the failure of many of the projects they fund. This implies that they are mainly funding projects which are more or less certain to bring in the predicted results. You need to reassure such donors that your project is one of those that will bring in results, even if it is pioneering and innovative.

Fundraising is about building a partnership between two organisations who share the same objectives. The partnership operates by you doing the work and the funder giving the financial support. So you are not begging for money; you are trying to engage someone with your work.

- What is their **grant range**? What is a typical grant for a project similar to your own? Are you applying for an amount they can realistically give? For example, a grant-making trust with an income of over £10 million does not want to give its money away in grants of £100; that would be an administrative nightmare. Its usual minimum grant will be about £500. However, for a local trust with an income of £20,000, £500 would be quite a large grant. And £500 for a small local company would be a massive grant.

- Do they have **advisers** who can help you informally when you are writing your application. Some funders will even ask you first to submit draft proposals to an adviser who can assist with the application while remaining independent of the decision-making process.

- **Are there any connections** between you and the funder? Either a personal link, or because there are particular reasons why they should be interested in what you are doing. These connections may be apparent, or may require some research. For example, a fundraiser for a veterinary faculty discovered that a trustee of a grant-making trust was a former graduate of the university to which she was attached. The trustee had also studied veterinary science. The trustee was promptly invited to dinner. The grant came through soon after the dinner.

  Similarly, when you are writing to a company you should always make a connection between you and the company you are writing to. Do you have a personal link (a member of their staff volunteers for your organisation, the chair of your management committee is the company managing director's bridge partner), a geographical link (you and the company operate in the same area and your users are their customers) or a product link? If you can't create a link, don't bother writing to that company.

- **What is the applications procedure**? In particular, how should applications be presented and when are the deadlines for receipt?

Benefits to the donor

Another aspect of donor research is establishing whether the donor might expect something in return for making the grant. In this context it is particularly important to understand the difference between sponsorship and a donation.

Sponsorship provides a direct benefit to the donor, which is the prime reason for giving support in the first place. Direct benefits include promotion and publicity, entertainment facilities and other services of commercial benefit to the sponsor.

With a donation, a donor should not normally require any significant direct benefit. Rather they should support the project because they believe it to be socially valuable. But it is important to be aware of some ways in which a donation can bring an *indirect* benefit to the donor. This can affect the way in which the proposal is presented. For example, the project might do the following.

- **Provide publicity** for the donation and/or identify the donor closely with the project that is being supported. Both provide recognition for the donor's contribution. This is especially important to companies and the National Lottery distribution boards. It is also attractive to grant-making trusts if you write up the results of the project and disseminate these. The trust is then seen as funding pioneering work and promoting best practice.
- **Deal with a problem that the donor is also concerned with**. This enables the donor to achieve something without actually having to do anything (except give you the money).
- **Provide a better or cheaper service**. The donor feels they are getting a good return on their money. On the basis that they have a grants budget which has to be spent, you are enabling them to spend their money more cost-effectively.

It is most important that you offer companies a benefit from their donation, whether it be better staff relations (if they support their employees' voluntary activity), a better name in the community (but show how are you going to achieve this), a good night out for staff, or whatever.

Irrespective of the level of benefit offered to or expected or required by the donor, there are some things you should do with all donors:

- **thank them** profusely and often
- **report back** regularly, showing them all the good things their donation has achieved
- **invite them** to open days and events
- **introduce them** to your patron, VIPs, users, etc.

This is not only good manners and an investment in a possible future grant, it also gives them a warm glow of satisfaction and a feeling of involvement.

8 WRITING A GOOD APPLICATION

There are no golden rules for writing a proposal. It is very much a matter of personal style and temperament. What works for one person will not necessarily work for another. And what works for you is what you should pay attention to. You may be able to get away with a piece of rhetoric or an impassioned plea for funds in your own handwriting, or only a very brief statement of your plans.

The suggestions that follow are meant as guidelines only. You can reject all of the ideas or pick up on those that seem useful to you. What is important is that you should write an application that you are happy with, that does justice to the work of your organisation and you feel is the best way to persuade someone to support you.

Presenting your work to funders – two golden rules

1 You cannot tell them everything. There isn't time and they wouldn't listen.
  So you have to select the points that donor is going to be most interested in.

2 In general, don't ask funders to support your organisation.
  Rather, ask them to support the people you help or the work you do.

The form of the application

Applications take several forms.

- **An application form supplied by the donor**. This will tell you precisely what information to supply. Use this format when required to do so. You might also wish to attach a covering letter or supporting information, although your case is likely to be judged on what you have put in the form.

  Some application forms are extremely detailed. The National Lottery Community Fund's form, for example, has over 20 pages. Just because you are filling out a form doesn't mean that you switch off your fundraising brain. Try to communicate the important needs you are meeting, your effectiveness in meeting them and the cost-effectiveness of your approach.

- **An application letter** in which you set out your case and attach supporting information as required. This format will be appropriate in most circumstances and is covered in detail in this chapter.

- **A project proposal and a covering letter**, together with supporting information. This follows on from the above. Dividing the application into two parts, a project proposal and a letter, has certain advantages. The letter can contain personal information – previous contact with the donor, particular reasons why the donor might be interested, as well as a brief project summary. The project proposal will be more formal and factual; the letter more up-beat, selling the idea of support. This format is especially useful for longer applications or where you are sending a standard proposal to a large number of donors. However, there is the danger that you can use it as an excuse to provide too much information, and that not everyone will read enough of the proposal to get a proper picture.

The information you supply will be assessed by the grants secretary, trust director, corporate affairs manager (or whoever) and put forward as a summary and recommendation to the grants committee or trustees, who will then make the decision. This is the most usual procedure for all but the smallest grant sources. So, your letter and other beautifully constructed prose may well not be read by the people making the final decisions. All they may see is a summary of your proposal. Therefore, you must make a good, clear case which can be easily understood and summarised.

A suggested structure for an application letter

- Project title
- Proposal summary
- Introduction: who you are
- The problem or need
- What you will do
- How you will do it
- How you will know if you've been successful
- How much you need to do it
- How you will get the money
- The request
- Why the donor might be interested
- Where the money will come from in the future
- Signing off

The structure of the application

Whatever form of proposal you actually produce, it has to fulfil certain functions. It has to inform the reader of who you are and what you intend to do, and it also has to say how much money you need and what you intend to spend it on. It should do this in a clear and logical way. Some of the elements you might use in constructing your proposal are detailed below:

1 The title

It is often a good idea to give your proposal a title, particularly if you can do this in a catchy phrase which captures the essence of what you want to do.

2 A summary

For a longer proposal, a summary can be very important. It presents the essence of what the proposal is about, and allows the reader to determine whether it is likely to be of interest. The summary may be presented in a covering letter, or the first paragraph of the application letter itself. It should be clear, concise and specific. It should describe who you are, the scope of your project, and the projected cost. The summary is the first part of your proposal that will be read, and it may be the last! Make sure that you follow the normal fundraising rules, even in the summary paragraph. Be positive and upbeat and state that something really good will happen as a result of this project.

Key question

Who are this lot – and can I trust them?

3 The introduction: who you are

This is the section of a proposal where you say who you are. Many proposals tell little or nothing about the applicant organisation and speak only about the project or programme to be conducted. If you are a nationally known organisation, you can state who you are in a line or a sentence. Usually you need to provide more information than this. Proposals are often funded on the basis of the reputation of the applicant organisation and its key people, as well as on the basis of the proposed project. The introduction is the section in which you build your credibility as an organisation which deserves to be supported.

Here are some of the things you can say about your organisation in your introduction.

- What **connection** with the funding source you have had in the past. Whether you have had a grant before, or applied and been turned down.

- Your organisation's **goals or objectives** and the basic thrust of your work.
- How you **got started**.
- **How long** you have been around.
- **Anything unique** about the way you got started, or the fact that you pioneered a new type of activity.
- Some of your **most significant accomplishments** as an organisation, or, if you are a new organisation, some of the significant accomplishments of your staff in their previous roles.
- What **support you have received** from other organisations and prominent individuals (accompanied perhaps by letters of endorsement which can be put in an appendix).

You are not putting down history for the sake of history, rather you are doing this to build your credibility. You are trying to show that you are a safe pair of hands, that you are (hopefully) an imaginative and exciting organisation to be associated with, and that you will continue to deliver a high quality of service.

Key question

Who are their users – and what is their (the users') problem?

4 The problem statement or assessment of need: why something needs to be done

In the introduction you have said who you are. Now you will home in on the specific problems that you want to solve through the project you are proposing.

Applicants often make the mistake of painting too broad a picture of all the ills plaguing people, the local community or the wider world. They do not narrow down to specific problems that are solvable. They give the impression that it will take a hundred times the requested budget even to begin to deal with the problems that have been identified. This is overkill. You may need to confine your definition of the problem so as to allow you to propose a solution. You are then showing how you will make a positive impact within a reasonable amount of time and with reasonable resources.

Another common problem is that applicants bang on about themselves and their needs. *'The community centre roof is falling in so please help us put a new one on.' 'Our play equipment is all broken and our subs don't cover the replacement cost.' 'Our staff are overworked.'* Although these may be the real reasons why you are fundraising, always present your proposals on the basis of your users, their needs, their hopes and aspirations.

Alternatively, applications can concentrate simply on the service that the applicant wants to provide rather than the reason why it wants to provide it. The letter launches in with something like: '*We want to provide a desperately needed new information line for at risk women*' and then explain in great detail how the service will be provided, managed and financed – but at no point explaining why there is a need for the service in the first place, and the really important changes the service will help make in the lives of those using it.

You need to document the problem. How do you know that a problem really exists? As the National Lottery Community Fund assessor's manual puts it: '*Has the organisation identified all possible beneficiaries and analysed their needs? For instance, has the organisation taken care to consider the whole range of people who could benefit from the project? Is there some evidence of need, such as a survey or enquiries from potential beneficiaries? Does the organisation demonstrate a good understanding of the range of beneficiaries' needs?*'

Furthermore, Don't just assume that everybody knows this is a problem. Use your own or other people's information to strengthen your case. For example, which of the following do you think is more convincing:

- 'It stands to reason that children whose parents cannot read or write will do badly at school'
- 'A recent Joseph Rowntree Foundation report on growing up with parents who have learning difficulties showed conclusively that "*children's destinies are not fixed by having a mother or father with learning difficulties*". The report went onto argue that ...'

Assume that the funder is intensely sceptical about the need for your project. What can you do to prove them wrong? The National Lottery Community Fund certainly will want hard evidence of the need for your project – bland assertions and generalised statements will not get past them.

Notwithstanding the above, don't go overboard and fill your proposal with tables, charts and graphs. These will interfere with the flow of the argument. Figures are only helpful if they support an argument being made. If you must use extensive statistics, put them in an appendix, but put the key figures into your statement of the problem.

When explaining why something needs to be done now, you need to do the following:

- Make a **logical connection** between your organisation's background and the problems and needs with which you propose to work.
- Support the existence of the problem by **evidence**. Statistics are one type of evidence. You may also get advice from groups in your community

concerned about the problem, from prospective clients, from other organisations working in your community and from professionals in the field.

- Define clearly **the problems** with which you intend to work.
- Make sure that what you want to do is **workable**, that it can be done within a reasonable time, by you, and with a reasonable amount of money.
- Show how something must be done now. If you can't give the application a **sense of urgency**, the funder will turn to one of the many which can.

Key question

What do they want to do to make life better for their users?

5 Your objectives: what you intend to do about the problem

Clearly if you have defined a problem then your proposals should offer some relief to the problem. Show that you have a clear plan to address the problems and issues you have already highlighted. Try also to set yourselves targets for what you propose to do so that you can give the funder a clear idea of what will happen and when. To quote from the Community Fund manual again: '*Does the project have clear and realistic objectives? For instance, is there a simple explanation of the project that makes it clear that the organisation knows exactly what is wants it wants to do? Can the objectives be achieved within the timescale suggested?*'

If the problem which you identify is a high incidence of vandalism by young people in your community (substantiated, of course), then an objective of your programme should be the reduction of the incidence of vandalism among the youth in your community. If the problem is long-term unemployment, then an objective is getting the long-term unemployed into jobs.

Distinguish between objectives (what you aim to achieve) and methods (how you will do it – *see opposite*). If you are having difficulty in defining your objectives, try projecting your organisation a year or two into the future. What differences would you hope to see between then and now? What changes will have occurred? These changed dimensions may be the objectives of your programme.

Also, and crucially, try to show that your users –or the intended beneficiaries of the project – have had a major input into developing the ideas and plans for the project. Have they been involved from the outset, or has there just been a token consultation towards the end?

It is worth examining your objectives in a little more detail. Some programmes may create very temporary jobs for people and attract those who are best able to find work by themselves. Even if they reduce the unemployment problem in the short term, after a year or two the problem will be back, as bad or worse than ever. You should be concerned about the quality of your work as well as the quantity (which is just the number of people you are helping).

Be as precise as you can in describing who you are helping and the severity of the problems being tackled, the extent of the service being provided, and the impact on those you are helping. For example:

In 40% of the households in XXX area there is no wage earner. Attendance on training and further education courses is Y% lower than the national average. The majority of these families are locked into a cycle of debt and dependence on benefits (Z% of households have had no private income coming into the home for over two years).

Our pilot project showed how we can help people break out of this cycle. As a result of the XXX Initiative, P% of those attending were still in training or education after six months and Q% had already found full or part-time work. As a result, their household income has risen by R%. More importantly, they now feel the have control over their own lives and futures.'

You can take it further to demonstrate the cost-effectiveness and value for money your project represents. Many grant-makers are now judging applications on the impact or outcome of the work and the value for the money they are putting up.

Set specific targets for the project. On the above example you could say something like: *'By the end of the three-year project, we expect a further W people to have gone through our X programme. Of these, Y will then go onto formal job training or into further education and Z will be in full or part-time work.'* This will give you a clear basis to measure the success of your work and reassure the funder that the project is well planned and thought through.

Key question

How do I know that it will work?

6 The methods: how you will attempt to do it

You have already stated who you are, the problem you want to work with, your objectives (which promise a solution to or reduction of the problem). Now you are going to explain how you intend to bring about these results.

You will need to describe the methods you will use and the activities you will conduct to accomplish your objectives. You will also need to persuade the funder that they will work. You can do this by demonstrating that:

- this project is **based on a successful model** developed elsewhere;
- the **outputs appear plausible**;
- it is a **natural extension** of work you have already undertaken, so it is not some great leap in the dark;
- it **fits well** with your organisation's other activities;
- you have **successfully managed projects** like this in the past;
- you have **experienced and well-qualified people** to run the project;
- you have the **support and commitment of the users**, and that they have been involved in the project's planning;
- it has the **backing of key people and agencies**, which can act as a kind of independent verification of the project plan;
- it is **clearly thought through** with clear targets and review processes at regular intervals;
- the work you have done in the past gives confidence that this new project is **well within your capabilities**.

The informed donor may want to know why you have selected these methods, particularly for an innovative project. This requires you to know a good deal about other projects of a similar nature. Who else is working on the problem and where? What methods have been tried in the past, and what are being tried now, and with what results? In other words, can you justify or substantiate your approach?

Key question

How will they know whether they are being successful?

7 Monitoring and evaluation: how you will measure performance

A key element of modern voluntary sector management –as well as one of the most important concerns for funders – is that of monitoring and evaluation. Put simply, being busy is not enough; funders want to know that you are being effective.

Basically, monitoring is about getting information; evaluation is making decisions in the light of this information. Monitoring can take many forms – interviews, questionnaires, surveys, consultation meetings, etc. Evaluation generally requires a manager or, more usually, a group of people to look at the feedback you get from your monitoring, assessing the points and issues it raises, and deciding whether you need to do anything differently.

From a funder's viewpoint, there are three key issues in the monitoring and evaluation process:

- That you are taking user comment and feedback very seriously. Just as you have involved users in defining the need and drawing up the project proposal, you also need to show that you will be involving them in the on-going management and development of the project. It is not enough just to assume that because you haven't had many complaints that things are going OK, or that because you are getting enough people along then you must be providing a good service. Funders want to see that you will be actively seeking out verification of all of this.
- That you don't just carry on regardless. Despite your best endeavours, things don't always turn out as you planned. You need to show that you will be able to stay on top of people and events, and respond to situations as they develop rather than trying to make everything fit a pre-determined model. Monitoring and evaluation processes give you this reality check.
- That the knowledge and information gathered as you run the project will be fed into the development of the project and, indeed, the wider organisation. You will be learning lots of really valuable information both about the way in which you work and the on-going needs of your users; you want to show how all of this will feed into your project and organisational planning.

Monitoring and evaluation isn't about screwing you down to the last penny, or ensuring that you deal with exactly the same number of people in exactly the same way as you said you were going to in your funding proposal (although there is an important element of accountability in all this). Funders would much rather that you were clear in what you are trying to achieve, but also honest in your assessment of performance. If it becomes clear that you should be doing things in a slightly different way than originally envisaged, then tell the funders how you have learned these lessons and why a modified approach would deliver better results for you and your users. They are usually happy to agree to their money being used in a slightly different way if it means the end results are more likely to be achieved.

You need to tell the funder how you intend to gather information during the course of the project and how you will evaluate it. For larger funding applications, it can often be worth setting up a small project steering committee drawing in the organisation, some partner agencies and some users. Basically, you need to show that:

- you will be obtaining **useful and reliable information**;
- this information will **inform the development of the project**;
- any **problems will be identified early** and will be acted upon;

- **user comment and criticism** will be sought out and used as a key management and development tool.

Key question

How much is it going to cost?

8 The budget: how much you will need to do this work

Fundraising is really about selling an idea rather than asking for money. It is primarily about showing how you can change things for the better. However, once you have sold the idea to someone with the means and inclination to support you, you then need to get down to the business of asking for money.

The budget is simply a statement of what you intend to spend on the project. It will include the direct project expenditure and possibly an allocation of overhead costs. In the application you may want to give a total budget figure, or you might break it down into smaller items according to what you think the particular donor is interested in (for example a particular project, idea or piece of equipment). Either way, the budget should show how the whole thing fits together. *See Chapter 5 on Costing a Project for more information.*

Be confident about money. If you have shown that you are a good organisation, that you are responding to an important need, and you are responding to this need in a sensible and appropriate way, that the funder can take further confidence from your excellent track record and experience of doing this kind of work, and that you can point to a well-costed budget – then if that is what the project costs, then that is what it costs. Don't be apologetic for asking for the money you need to do a good job. Tell it how it is. When looking at a budget funders will consider issues such as whether:

- the budget has been calculated in a clear and logical way that has taken **all relevant costs** into account;
- it has been put together by someone who **understands the problem**;
- it is **based on experience** of budgeting for other projects;
- the **costs are reasonable** for this type of work and will allow you to provide a good level of service.

As the Community Fund puts it: '*Are you [the assessor] confident that they have not budgeted in such a way that will compromise quality?*'

If you are applying for a grant over several years, inflation can pose a problem. There are two ways of tackling this. Firstly, you can allow for inflation at a guessed rate; secondly you can compute your own budget at present costs and ask for an inflation allowance to be added each year according to the prevailing level. In the present economic climate with low inflation rates, this is less of an issue and it is probably best to allow for inflation. If you are in doubt, consult the funder as they may have specific ways of dealing with this.

Key question
Where are they getting the money from?

9 Funding plan

If you are only applying to a donor for part of the money you need, explain where you intend to obtain the balance. The funder will be asking two key questions:

- **What is their track record in fundraising?** What does this tell me about their ability to get money for this project? For example, if you have raised around £50,000 a year from grant-making trusts for the last six years and you are currently seeking support for a £30,000 project, the donor you are writing to will be pretty confident in your ability to raise the full amount and will contribute accordingly. If you have never raised a penny and now expect to get £100,000 over the next year, this looks like wishful thinking unless you can make a convincing case otherwise.
- **Who else has put money in?** The more money you have raised or had promised from elsewhere, the more confidence this funder will have in your ability to get the project fully funded.

If you are applying for a piece of equipment or a capital project, it's not just a matter of showing how you can raise the money to buy the equipment. You must also demonstrate that you have the resources to use it. Donors don't like paying for a building or an expensive piece of equipment only to find it lying idle as you can't afford to use it. You need to demonstrate how you intend to meet these running costs.

Key question
How much do they want from us?

10 The request: how much to ask for

At this stage, many applications tail off into a murmur that any contribution would be gratefully received. This is partly due to an embarrassment about asking for money. It also stems from a lack of confidence about exactly how much to ask for.

But going back to first principles, fundraising is about making a good case, selling a cause. Once the case is made and the importance of the project is accepted by the donor, making a grant is something that is done willingly because the donor wants to help.

The only question is how much to give. Here it can be helpful to the donor if you make a specific request rather than ask them to decide what is appropriate. Of course, before you do this you need to know how much the donor is able to give – the total amount they have to give and a typical size of grant made in the past to similar organisations for similar purposes. Then you can assess the likely grant range which this donor might consider and ask for a specific amount. You can make this suggestion in a number of ways:

- **ask directly for a specific sum** (*'I would like to ask you for a one-off grant of £5,000'*, or *'Could you support us with £2,500 for three years'*, or whatever)
- **show how much other trusts have given or has been committed** (*'The Garfield Weston Foundation has already given us £10,000'*). This will indicate that you expect a similar amount from the trust you are currently writing to
- **say how many trusts you are writing to and for how much** (*'I am writing to you and nine other trusts asking for a total of £42,000'*). This again gives the donor an idea of how much you are expecting them to give (£5,000–£10,000 in this example), but also gives them flexibility. You can even append a list of the donors you are approaching. They may know one another and discuss your application and the contribution each might make if they are particularly impressed with it
- **provide a shopping list** (£12,000 for the project itself, £3,000 for the research, £3,000 for the publication, £2,000 for the evaluation etc.). They can then chose what to support, based on their preferences and budget.

The other thing you need to do is show the funder how their grant fits into the overall picture. So you need to say how much you need in total, where it is coming from and what you expect that donor to give. For example: *'We need to raise £210,000. Our members have already committed £60,000 and the health authority has agreed to match this amount. We expect to raise a further £40,000 from fundraising events, £20,000 from local and national companies and £30,000 from grant-making trusts. I am therefore writing to ask you for ...'*. This will give the funder more confidence that you know what you are doing and that you can raise the necessary money.

11 The rationale: why the donor might be interested

There are many reasons why the donor might be interested in your proposal:

- you are running a **good project** which falls **within their stated policies** and priorities
- you have **already received a grant** from them, and a further grant is an investment in your success
- they have **a known interest** or some particular connection with the problem or cause
- there is a **personal connection** which it will pay to highlight
- there is a **payback** for them in the form of good publicity.

Whatever the reason, you may want to mention it in the application (or the covering letter or a conversation with the donor). This is particularly important when you are approaching a company who will be wanting to know what PR or other commercial benefit they will get from their support.

12 Where will the money come from in future?

Another important consideration is what you intend to do when the grant you are seeking runs out. Is your project time-limited, say three years or less? If so, you don't have to worry about getting funding beyond then. However, often you are trying to get a new project going on the basis that if it works you will want it to continue for as long as necessary (and certainly beyond three years). Given that most funders will not give grants for more than three years, what happens when their funding runs out?

You need to think about this at the outset, as no funding source wants to be locked into supporting a project for ever. One way used to be to get a commitment from a statutory authority to take over the project once it had proved itself; but with cutbacks in public spending, this has become increasingly difficult, if not impossible. So what are the options?

- If the statutory authority will not definitely commit itself to funding the whole project, then they may at least indicate a willingness to consider a funding application if the project proves successful.

- You may be able to show that the project fits in with a statutory service's priorities and that you expect to be able to run it on a contract basis.
- The project may generate an income of its own (for example you can build in a charging structure to users or another body which will grow to cover the project's costs within the life span of the grant).
- You are developing your general fundraising or income-generating activities and expect to be able to pay for the project from within your own resources – or at least a substantial proportion of the costs.
- Over the lifetime of the grant you will be aiming to double your membership to bring in an additional £X a year into your organisation. Some of this can be transferred to paying for the project from year four onwards.

It may well be that you use a combination of the above, or have some other scheme of your own. The key thing to do is think about it now and show the funder that you are planning ahead. You may not be certain that you will be able to obtain funding in the way you suggest, but at least you will have thought about the problem at an early stage and provided some reassurance to those who would like to fund you.

Also, it gives you a fundraising plan to be getting on with.

In fact, many funders like the idea of giving grants on a tapering basis – for example £15,000 in year 1, £12,000 in year 2 and £8,000 in year 3. As their grant goes down other money comes into the project. Asking for money on this basis can help show that you are confident of bringing in this additional money, and that in turn gives the funder confidence in the long-term viability of your work.

As the old National Lottery Charities Board used to put it: *'Assure us that your organisation has a sensible plan to secure new sources of funding if the project is expected to continue when our grant has expired'*.

13 The signatory: who puts their name to the application

Who signs the letter can be important. If the applicant is recognised or known to the donor, this can be helpful. The following are possible signatories:

- the **project leader**
- the **fundraiser** or development officer
- the organisation's **director**
- the **chair of the trustees** or management committee
- an **appeal patron**
- an **expert** or **prominent personality** with some connection with the cause.

Who is the best person for the job depends very much on the nature of the body you are approaching. It is up to you to decide who will be the best signatory to the application. But beware the following.

- You write saying that you are doing so at the suggestion of a prominent person (connected with you and known to them). This can imply that that person is too busy to be able to or to want to make the application in person.

- Follow up information and contact will be with another person. This again implies that the person signing the letter is too important or too busy to be concerned with following it up. As a general principle any signatory should be prepared, at least, to attend a follow-up meeting with the donor (diary permitting) to discuss the grant.

- The signatory has a job title which appears too junior – fundraising assistant or assistant to the director, for example. Again, this implies that you are not treating the application seriously. If you are given the responsibility for signing the letter and your job title is inadequate, then get promoted – or at least get it agreed that you can use a more appropriate job title when signing fundraising letters.

- The signatory is a fundraising consultant acting on your behalf. There are two problems here:
  (i) the consultant will almost certainly become a Professional Fundraiser under the terms of the Charities Act and will have to make some rather clumsy-looking declarations about how they are being paid for their work.
  (ii) many funders refuse to consider appeals from a third party on behalf of a charity. Even if they don't rule you out on these grounds, donors respond best to direct requests, even though the approach may have been put together with professional advice.

The length of the application

You cannot tell donors everything. You haven't got time and they won't read it. You just need to tell them enough. It is difficult enough reading thirty applications each day, every day – which is what many donors have to do. Put yourself in their position. You would pick up an application, look at who it was from, read the first paragraph and then possibly decide that the application was really worth bothering with. If you did read all of it, you may skip through much of the text simply because there was so much to read.

On the other hand, if it was clear, to the point and brief it would be so much easier to absorb the information. Donors are not paying you for the words you write. So you don't have to provide a lot of words to get a lot of money.

Key points

The main points to remember in any application are:

- build the credibility of your organisation
- support the need for your proposed project
- develop clear, specific, measurable and attainable objectives
- justify your approach
- include methods for evaluating your progress
- show how your future funding will go
- use simple, clear, understandable language – avoid jargon and rhetoric
- say it concisely and briefly
- prepare a realistic budget and include all relevant costs.

The ingredients of a good application – a summary

The application should be addressed to a named individual at the funding body. It could contain all of the following:

- Proposal title, a catchy phrase encapsulating the essence of what you propose to do.
- Proposal summary (or covering letter) for a longer application highlighting the key points.
- Introduction explaining who you are, what you do and why you're wonderful.
- Problem statement or assessment of need, showing why something needs to be done now.
- Project objectives explaining what you intend to do and the outcome you expect.
- Method describing how you intend to set about undertaking the project.
- Monitoring and evaluation describing how you intend to plot your progress and effectiveness.
- Budget showing the resources you need to carry out the work.
- Funding plan showing how you intend to set about raising the money.
- Request asking the donor to make a contribution (of a specified amount)
- Rationale for the donation stating why you believe it appropriate for the donor to say yes. This could be included in the covering letter.
- The longer term, saying where the money will come from in the future (if you want the project to continue) and what else you expect to come out of the project.
- Signing off mentioning the information you are attaching to the application, and suggesting who to contact for further information or to arrange a project visit. Who signs the letter can also be important.
- Back up information to support your application.

Nor is it a case of 'never mind the quality, feel the width'. You have to show what you are doing, give evidence that it is an exciting project that meets a real and important need, and that you can make an impact.

- Try to keep the application to two pages for a grant-making trust and one page for a company. This means that it can be easily photocopied and stands less chance of being summarised and possibly misrepresented by someone else. Obviously, for a very major project you might want to go into more detail, but here you can write a much shorter summary proposal.
- If in doubt, leave it out. Each point must add something to the case you are making. If it doesn't, it is making a negative impact by obscuring those parts of the application that do.
- You can always supply more detail in an attachment, although this may not be read. Or you can indicate that further information is available on request, which they will seldom ask for. Or they will ask to meet you; any discussion will generate far more useful and revealing information about the proposal and your competence than anything you put in writing.

> Don't rely on the attachments. Assume the only things the funder reads are the letter and budget. They should have a full understanding of who you are, what you want to do, why it's important and what it will cost. If you keep writing in the letter 'For further information see attached', they probably won't.

Back-up information

You might want to include any or all of these:

- Your organisation's **annual report and accounts**, or a leaflet containing the information in an abridged form (this would include photographs of your work wherever possible).
- A **detailed budget** for the project.
- A **detailed plan** for the project.
- **Visual material**, such as photographs of the project in action or architectural drawings for a building project.
- A **background briefing** on the need for the project (to include key statistics which bolster your case).
- A **case study** or several examples of the problem or what you can achieve.
- A **list of donors** and contributors.
- A **fundraising plan** (where and who you intend to get the money from).
- **Curriculum Vitae** of the key personnel involved in the project.
- A **list of trustees**, patrons, vice-presidents or other key supporters.

- **Letters of endorsement** from prominent people/other funders/users/ beneficiaries.
- A **quotes sheet** where users, community leaders and other notables say really positive things about you.
- Photocopies of **press cuttings**.

Always attach a budget for the project, an annual report and set of accounts. Over and above that, think what the donors will want to know, and what they will need to know before they give their support. Don't overload the system by sending everything. This is a waste of money, a waste of paper, and it will cost more to post. And, they won't all be photocopied for the trustees or grants committee members.

All attachments are fundraising documents. The same rules which apply to writing your fundraising letter apply to the attachments (short sentences, easy to read, lots of sub headings, etc.). If they are not easy to read or are packed with jargon, either re-write them or leave them out.

9 SENDING YOUR APPLICATION

What to do with your application

Once you've written your application, you then need to think about and plan how, when and to whom to send it. You may have targeted a number of potentially interested sources and need several grants to make up the total cost of the project. Who should you approach first? And for how much? How can you maximise your chances of meeting your fundraising target? And how can you make sure that you raise the money you need within often tight deadlines?

There are no specific answers to these questions. It is as much a matter of your judgement and style as anything else. But the following points may help.

1 Apply immediately

Applications for small sums to the smaller trusts can be sent out whenever you like. Many of these trusts meet infrequently (often only once or twice a year), and it may be some time before you hear the outcomes of your appeal. So the sooner you get these applications out, the better.

However, small local grants can be very useful in levering out large national ones. The fact of the endorsement is probably more useful to you than the amount of money they give, as it gives confidence to the national trust that those on the ground know, like and trust you (*see below*). But remember the national trust will only know you have got local money if you tell them!

2 The blanket approach

Suppose you have identified 30 sources as being potentially interested in your work; you might then send out all 30 applications at once. The advantage of this is that you will have actually asked 30 people to support you; and they can then decide whether to do so or not. The disadvantage is that your appeal may not be as strong as where you adopt the step-by-step approach (*discussed below*).

In your application, you might state that you are approaching a number of sources, and even name some of them. You might try to indicate in some way how much you would like each to give (for example '*We are writing to you and eight other major trusts asking for a total of £30,000*').

Some donors will not reply. Some will acknowledge receipt of your application, and that will be the last you hear. Some will want further information. A few might request a meeting. Some will simply send you a cheque, if your application is successful.

You can use their response to improve your chances. If one of your top prospects says '*no*', it may be worth politely finding out why, possibly asking for a meeting or a visit so that you can explain the importance of your work in greater depth. There are many instances of an applicant being able to turn a '*no*' into a '*yes*' in this way. In any case, you will begin to accumulate information about their approach to grant-making which will improve your chances of success next time around.

If you have been successful, you can send a follow-up letter to some of the other trusts that have not yet reached a decision, outlining the progress of the appeal. This can remind them that your appeal is outstanding, as well as give them further information which might enhance your chances.

If you fall just short of your target, don't just keep trying to find yet another untapped source of money. Go back and ask a few of your key supporters – say how successful you have been and see if there is the possibility of topping up their support with a further small grant.

> Fundraising is not 'fair'. The more you raise, the easier it is to raise more. Therefore, trumpet your success to funders, especially those who have not yet decided whether to give you a grant.

3 The step-by-step approach

Here you identify from your list of potential sources a few which you believe are more likely to be interested in you and which have the resources to make a substantial grant. If you are applying for a large grant from a statutory source, it is always important to do this first, and to get some commitment before approaching others for support. The statutory grant can be the key component in your fundraising plan, and other donors may want to be assured that you have got what you can out of statutory rather than charitable funds.

How you approach your major donors will depend on their application procedures, how well you are known to them and whether they have supported you previously. You may be able to arrange a meeting to discuss your proposal; you may want to find out first about the grant cycle, when applications are due in and when they will be considered.

Most of the major grant-making trusts are based in London and the South-East of England. That's fine if you are also based there, but most of us aren't. So before writing to a national trust based in London check to see if there are any local trusts who you can approach first. They may be big, they may be small. However, the point is not necessarily to get huge sums from them; rather, you are simply trying to say to the London-based trust, in effect: '*You may not have heard of us because we are not based in your area. However, the XXX Trust which is based in our area and is in a position to know thinks we are marvellous, because they have just given us £1,000. Therefore you, the distant trust, can take confidence from this donation.*' Obviously you don't actually write this! The grant from a local trust is acting like a letter of reference.

Taking this a stage further, there are some trusts with a regional structure – notable the Lloyds TSB Foundation for England & Wales, the Esmée Fairbairn Charitable Trust and the BBC Children in Need Appeal. They have regional offices and regional administrators. Again, it is often worth contacting these trusts earlier rather than later in the process to see if they will commit to giving you a grant. A grant from Lloyds TSB Foundation, for example, will be very helpful in persuading other national foundations to support you. These national foundations will know that Lloyds TSB will have assessed you using their regional administrators. It's not quite a case of '*if it's good enough for Lloyds TSB then it's good enough for us*', but – as the saying goes – '*every little helps*'!

More and more funders are operating what is, in effect, a pledge system. They commit to giving you a certain sum on money on the understanding that the total sum is raised by a certain date. It is fairly straightforward for you to operate a similar system. You can write along the lines of: '*We are aiming to raise a total of £75,000 by September 2003. Will you commit to giving £10,000 on the basis that the total sum is raised by then?*'

They don't actually send you the £10,000 until you can confirm that you have raised the other £65,000. However, you can use their commitment to obtain similar pledges from other funders: '*We are aiming to raise a total of £75,000 by September 2003. We have already firm commitments of support totalling £40,000. We therefore only need a further £35,000. Will you commit to giving £10,000 on the basis that the total sum is raised by September 2003?*'

Do all you can to get your large grants committed. Once you have got your first grant, everything then becomes much easier. Your target is reduced; you have an endorsement for what you are doing; and your confidence grows. This makes it more likely that others will agree to support you.

Whatever you do make sure that for each approach you mention something of your fundraising strategy. Ask for support at a specific level and put this into the context of your overall fundraising plans for the project. Tell them who has already supported you. Tell them who else you are approaching. Suggest to them that their 'lead' grant might encourage others to give to you. In other words, you will be able to write: '*We need a total of £30,000 from grant-making trusts. The XXX Foundation has already given a grant of £8,000, so now we only need a further £22,000. Therefore, I am writing to you and eight other major trusts asking for a total of £22,000.*'

In fundraising, you always quote the highest figure you need, showing how much has been raised and how much you still need.

4 The delayed approach

In most applications, you will be asking for money. But there are other possibilities. You can send an outline of your proposals and ask for a meeting to discuss your ideas. This is usually only worthwhile where you are already well-known to the donor, or where they have regional offices (like Lloyds TSB Foundation – *see above*) or have specialist advisers (like the Baring Foundation in Merseyside and Cornwall). Otherwise, funders normally prefer a full written proposal in the first instance.

You can try to get them to visit you. Open days, launches and other events can provide suitable opportunities for this. If you are organising a prestigious event, this can be a particularly appropriate time to get potential supporters to visit you. Some projects, such as City Farms, have a product which is inherently attractive to donors, and experience shows that most of the people who visit eventually decide to give financial support. In such circumstances, the challenge is to find ways of getting them to accept an invitation to visit you.

You can try to get yourself known in the grant-making world before you actually apply. This means:

- meeting grants administrators and advisers at **events and conferences**, and making sure you introduce yourself;
- sending out **your annual report** (for information purposes only) to potential supporters;
- seeking and **getting publicity** in the media;
- building your **trustee, patron or supporter base** so that you create wider contacts for your organisation.

It is hard to obtain substantial support for a project when you have never received support before. This may mean presenting more modest needs now, and building on this over time. It also means being very clear about which funders you are targeting over the next five years or so and making sure you think strategically about how you will do this.

What to do after the application

Mostly you will do nothing, except wait for a response. You can chase up your letter with a phone call to find out if it has arrived, when it will be considered, and whether they require any further information. This, at least, has the advantage of putting a human voice to a written application. But you do need to do this carefully. There is a danger of appearing to hassle them, which they will resent.

When you do receive a positive reply, say 'thank you' immediately. Put the donor on a mailing list to receive information on your work (such as annual reports and copies of the publications you produce). Note any conditions of the grant that have to be met (terms for spending the money, reporting and audit requirements, etc.).

Keep good records of your contacts. Add information from your refusals as well as your successes. They may give reasons for turning you down. Note these, as this can help you next time, although what they say may be out of politeness rather than the bare truth. When you do re-apply, remind them that you have applied before. Remember that the bodies that have supported you this time are quite likely to want to support you again (unless they have a specific policy of not doing so).

You should consider when and how next to approach them. As most grant-making bodies work on annual grant cycles, you may decide to go back for more support next year. As a rule, never apply to the same funder more than once in their financial year.

Anybody who has turned you down should be seen as a possibility for future support (unless there are clear reasons why they will never support you). You have decided that they are likely to be interested. The only problem is that they have not yet come to the same conclusion. It is your challenge to present a better case next time or even the time after. Persistence can pay.

A first application should be seen as the beginning, not the end, of the process. Success in raising money depends as much on building relationships and not giving up, as on writing a good application for a good project.

Fundraising takes time. The more time you leave the better. Try to plan at least a year ahead.

And when you receive a grant, think of this as the first of many instalments, not the one and only. Put time and energy into building the relationship.

Timing and timescale

One reason many applications fail is that they are made too late. The time to think about applying is well before you need the money. This means that planning ahead is vital. Raising money to extricate yourself from a financial crisis is by far the most difficult form of fundraising.

There are various stages in the application process, each with a time scale attached:

- **getting known** and getting to know potential supporters
- **building credibility** with a donor, so that they will be happy to give you a real grant rather than a token donation
- **developing your fundraising ideas** and completing a written application. This might include a process of discussion with potential donors
- **submitting a formal application**
- **assessing the application** and making a recommendation to the trustees or grants committee
- the **timescale for their decision** at a trustee or grants committee meeting
- **communication of the decision** to the applicant, which may require an acceptance by the applicant of the terms and conditions of the grant before the money can be paid over.

The first two stages can take many years, but time spent on building credibility is never wasted. The subsequent phases also take time. The trustees or grants committee may only meet quarterly and may require applications to be submitted at least one month in advance. The grants budget at the next trustee meeting may already be fully absorbed, and the applicant might only stand any real chance if the application is deferred until a subsequent meeting.

Organisations in receipt of local authority funding must apply in the late summer for grants for the year beginning the following May. And they may be wise to start preliminary discussions for the next year's grant at about the time that the current year's grant is confirmed.

Of course, there will always be emergencies or projects where the need was unforeseen which need to be funded immediately. The point here is that if you have already developed good relationships with potential funders, securing emergency funding is that much easier. Conversely, if you haven't done the preparatory work it is difficult and often impossible to get funded at short notice, however desperate the need.

10 WORKED EXAMPLES

This chapter analyses some genuine applications which have been sent to real funders. We aim to be constructively critical and suggest ways in which they could be improved. Each application letter is reproduced, although some have been slightly modified to disguise the true identity of the organisation. We also provide a commentary to highlight some key points.

There are a number of lessons to be gained from reading through these annotated examples:

- Once an application is written, it is often easy to improve on it. Read your first draft, get others to read it, and produce a much better second (and final) draft.
- Many applications that are sent are not particularly good. They are impersonal circulars, impassioned pleas without sufficient evidence to make a good case, a hotchpotch of half thought-through ideas; or they are sent to someone who is unlikely to be interested (the applications here are generally much better than most). Writing a good application gets you off to a good start.
- Read through a range of applications. That puts you in a similar position to a donor – you will have a lot to read about projects you know little about. Which would you fund if you had a limited grants budget at your disposal? Understanding the process from the donor's point of view can only be helpful.
- Finding the correct people to write to is as important as getting the message right.

All the examples shown here are good attempts by people working for successful projects that they believe in. We hope they take our comments in the positive context we intended!

Example 1 – Jargon will get you nowhere

This application comes from a very committed and low-cost project. It is also nice and short. However, sadly, it doesn't really tell you anything, or at least nothing that is substantiated. It is simply a series of assertions – generally in some kind of management speak – that leave the reader none the wiser.

25th January

Dear Secretary

We are writing to ask for a few minutes of your time to read of our work and of our aims and objectives for the challenging year ahead.

Our small charitable Foundation is trying to raise funds to enable us to both continue and enlarge projects already established around the World, also to break into new horizons where we feel we can make a difference to the lives of those who face poverty, disadvantage, and physical or mental distress and be an enabler in them achieving real improvement in the quality of their lives.

In short our Hopes and Dreams Projects aim to provide Skills Transfer and encourage Social Development. We have maintained a high degree of Local Empowerment, Ownership and Involvement and our innovative projects have realised significant benefits relative to outlay, on hand-over, each project has the initial grounding to become self-sustaining. Our Foundation has been on time with all targets set to date, and will endeavour to continue this example. Evaluation methods continue to be in place both before and after hand-over.

We have the necessary Management Structure and have an Equal Opportunities Statement and a Mission Statement in place. Computers have made it possible for mass production of letters such as this, but we do assure you our greatest wish is to be as personal as possible in every project we undertake giving each recipient of our services the respect and love they so richly deserve.

If you would like to see photographs of our 'special' people, both young and elderly, please do consider telephoning to speak to me, I would like the opportunity of speaking to you.

Finally, we do not employ computer wizards, and our office work is carried out voluntarily. Much time is spent on sorting letters, but human errors do occur, I do hope very much that you do not receive more than one letter, please forgive us if you do. Postage money has been donated. We really would appreciate any financial help that you may be able to give, no matter how small.

Yours very truly

Helen Bateman

For example, what does it mean 'to provide Skills Transfer and encourage Social Development'? Even if you get past the jargon of 'realised significant benefits relative to outlay', where is any evidence or illustration of any of the points made in paragraph three? Why should the funder trust you simply because you know your way around some voluntary sector catch phrases? Significantly, where is there any evidence of meaningful local partnership, the absolute essential of any non-UK work?

This letter will make complete sense to the person who wrote it, but to few others. It's always a good idea to give your application to someone outside your organisation to read before you send it off. It is very easy when you are committed to and know a lot about a subject to see it from the non-expert's perspective. Jargon can be the death of an application; it certainly is in this case.

Also, this letter is clearly a circular. The original has a photocopied signature – which is a bit of a giveaway – but the whole tone is impersonal. There is no mention of the funder, nor any indication as to why the application may be relevant to this trust. In fact, the letter admits it is a circular (in paragraph four), and doesn't really make any effort to counter the ill-effects of this in paragraph six. This kind of approach hardly works when mass-mailing members of the public; it certainly won't to grant-making bodies.

The basic tone of this letter is: 'I know this is impersonal to you [the funder], but please rest assured that we don't treat our "special people" this way'. Not the best way of making a funder feel valued and respected!

Example 2 – A wasted opportunity

Here is a letter to a company asking for prizes to be donated for the charity's spring draw. It has certain merits. For example:

- it is a good length
- it recognises the company's desire for publicity
- it tries to tie the charity in with the company by showing a geographical and personnel connection.

10th September

Dear Mrs Higgins

Each year we run an Autumn Draw in order to raise money for the work of *** Charity. The draw is one of our most important sources of income, enabling us to provide vital support, advice and help for the five million or so people of all ages in the UK with ***, including more than 12,000 children. We do this through our 650 branches; groups for young disabled people; hotels and residential homes; and counselling and information services. We have several branches in Merseyside [where the company is based] and many of your customers and staff will have a first hand knowledge of the disease.

As 1995 is our 50th anniversary, we will be holding a special Golden Anniversary Draw. Suitable prizes will be crucial to its success and as we rely on donations, if you could help us by donating a prize we would be extremely grateful.

We will, of course, acknowledge your generosity through press releases, our own newspaper, What's Going On? (the best-read publication of its type, going to 100,000 people) including a special souvenir edition, and acknowledgement on the 2 million tickets we will have printed (in mid-October).

In our 50th anniversary year, the combined activities of celebration, fundraising and campaigning at all levels will provide *** Charity and its sponsors with a significant boost to public awareness and support. We are planning several major activities that will generate considerable media interest.

Any help and support you could offer would be greatly appreciated.

Yours sincerely,

Richard H. Smibbs

Events & Exhibitions Manager

However, it could be so much better.

Firstly, this should be a very prestigious affair. A major celebratory year, potentially massive publicity across a wide cross-section of the population and lots of branches to ensure that the two million tickets are sold. Yet the letter is written just one month before the tickets are due to be printed. All this could have been sorted out well in advance. Furthermore, the whole thing should have been presented as a major sponsorship opportunity, rather than merely 'please donate a prize'.

Secondly, the funder has no real idea of the kind of prize required. How many are supposed to be awarded? What was given by whom last year? Did the charity have a particular company product in mind?

The letter says that the draw is a key part of the charity's fundraising. So how much does it raise? A lot of money, no doubt. Again, this could be a real selling point because at little cost to the company (missing out on one sale) the donation could help generate a massive amount of money. This could show terrific leverage.

There are some presentation problems. The first paragraph is very long and rather uninspiring. Why don't they get a user to say how wonderful the charity is or sign up a celebrity appeal patron to say the same thing – anything which makes the appeal a bit more exciting.

The third paragraph offers the company a range of benefits. Because they are all crammed into one sentence, they get a bit lost. Why not separate them out into bullet points?

The point of the fourth paragraph is not clear. Is the charity trying to offer the company further sponsorship opportunities? If so, what are they? Also, what is the centre-piece of the year of celebration (royal visit or whatever)? A carrot could be dangled about this.

Example 3 – Just because you've got problems ...

One of the key ideas in this book is that fundraising is about building confidence in the mind of the donor that your plans and ideas are worthwhile and that you can deliver the intended results. Therefore, the best fundraising is usually planned well ahead.

In reality, this is not always possible, and crisis fundraising has its place. However, even here the basic rules stay the same. You are still trying to build confidence in the mind of the donor that whatever has gone on in the past, the future remains bright and that you have sensible plans to get the organisation back on its feet.

Dear Mr Morris

South County Wildlife Trust – Impacts of foot and mouth disease

I am writing to ask for your financial support to help us recover from the impact of Foot and Mouth disease (FMD). Even though the disease has just been announced as being officially cleared, the Trust is still suffering from its disastrous after effects.

Since its foundation in 1962, the South County Wildlife Trust has become one of the country's most visionary nature conservation charities. Despite being based in the south, many of our projects are recognised as being of national importance. The aim of the Trust is to conserve and protect wildlife habitats and threatened species. This is achieved through the management of nature reserves, the large-scale restoration of rare habitats and by encouraging environmentally sustainable lifestyles through its wide-ranging education programme.

Foot and mouth disease has had serious implications for the South County Wildlife Trust. Ours was one of the first counties to be affected by the disease and much of our work was immediately paralysed. It has been estimated that the Trust will have lost up to one third of its core income as a result of the disease. At the end of this current financial year we are facing a deficit of £150,000 through no fault of our own.

During the summer we were forced to cancel all of our outdoor events, many of which attract the new members we so badly need to support our work. We also had to cancel the 'Murphy Trail', our largest annual fundraising event – a sponsored walk which normally raises over £30,000. This year it raised nothing at all!

In addition, the spread of FMD has set back our conservation work by at least a year. Without access to the countryside we could not check otter holts for signs of habitation, volunteers could not survey rivers for water voles, we could not even put up bird and bat boxes – thus many projects have over run their scheduled times and budgets.

Replacing lost income, repairing damage to reserves where possible and catching up on our work in the wake of foot and mouth will require extra funds. We have no way of replacing the income we have lost because of the FMD – even our normal fundraising events themselves fell victim to the outbreak.

Our only hope is to ask for your help. The South County Wildlife Trust rarely receives donations in excess of £200 and would therefore greatly welcome any donation to enable us to continue our vital conservation work.

We do hope you will be able to offer your support.

Yours sincerely

S. Cummerford

Fundraising Officer

This application was written at the end of December 2001, in the wake of the Foot and Mouth epidemic that had ravaged many parts of the countryside. There are various flaws in the application, many of which arise out of its introspective nature. Foot and Mouth was not the funder's fault; nor can the medium-sized trust that the application was sent to repair all the damage. Therefore, the application needs to make a convincing case for how it can recover from here. It fails to do this.

Paragraph two makes some typical assertions about how good the organisation is, but without any evidence. You would expect to see at least one example of its 'visionary' work, or allusions to specific projects which are deemed to be of 'national importance'. However, this is somewhat skated over in the rush to get to the key, bad news.

There is no doubt that the wildlife trust has suffered badly through Foot and Mouth, and nobody would seriously dispute that it was not to blame for this. Hence the 'through no fault of our own' is a bit over-stated. The real weakness, however, is not that the application is rather over-written (even though it is), but rather that it does not suggest any constructive way out of the problem.

The critical issue is not that the charity has been unable to raise any money, but that its work has suffered enormously as a result. Again, the application makes a very dangerous assumption, namely that the reader will understand all the issues involved. He or she won't. Therefore, why is it a problem that the trust has been unable to put up any bird and bat boxes, or survey the rivers for water voles? How will wildlife suffer as a result? These things need to be pointed out.

Furthermore, you cannot replace a lost year's work all at once. The application needs to be clear about what is the most urgent work that needs doing, and ask for money accordingly. Once that is done they can move onto the next piece. Also, they could even argue for help simply to get the fundraising back on track. Clearly they have been very successful in the past, but may well need extra investment to restore their fundraising strength.

As it stands the application basically reads: 'Help, we're desperate and it's not our fault!' To which the reply is something like: 'I'm sure you are and I'm sure it's not – but what are you actually going to do?' It is often the case that the times you are most in need of money is when you need to be at your most reassuring. Yes, you may have a problem and it may be serious; but you need to show a good, solid, deliverable plan to deliver a brighter future. This application fails to do this, even though the organisation clearly has an awful lot going for it.

Example 4 – Still say what you want

This is a very good application from an excellent project. It clearly meets a need and is a really good example of local people helping regenerate local communities. Being critical it is rather densely written and a bit repetitive. Some parts, such as the paragraph on the Community Legal Service being awarded a kite mark, could be dealt with much more quickly – in this case in a sentence or two. Getting the award is a good achievement, and helps build credibility, but that is all the application need say on the point.

19th December

Dear Mr Evans

We are writing to ask whether you might be able to assist us with grant aid.

Northtown Neighbourhood Advice Centre was established in 1986 to provide a free, confidential and independent service to the people of Northtown on a wide range of welfare rights issues, e.g. benefits, debt, housing, consumer. We offer advice in a variety of ways, (e.g. drop-in, appointments, home visits, telephone, letter, fax) thereby enabling us to give an extremely comprehensive and flexible service. The work of the Centre is primarily concerned with the alleviation of poverty and the issues surrounding deprivation and social exclusion. We are the only advice service in Northtown and one of the few in North County to offer drop-in sessions, which ensures that no client has to wait for more than two days to obtain advice/information. Last financial year we dealt with 5,168 clients and 12,853 queries (an 11% increase on the previous year).

The Centre is very much a community-based project and is managed by a local voluntary Management Committee. A large proportion of the local community relies upon the Centre for an extensive range of invaluable advice and information. The Centre has enormous support from the local community and is seen as a vital resource in a severely deprived area, which has high numbers of unemployed, disabled and elderly people. North County Council and government surveys have shown North County to rank as one of the most deprived areas in the UK with the poorest health in the country. Reliance on incapacity benefit is double the national average and morbidity and standard mortality rate data reveal that people die earlier in North County and suffer longer term limiting illness than most other areas of the country.

The prevalence of disability in North County is three times higher than the national average. The closure of the Centre, due to lack of funds, would deny thousands of vulnerable people the right to a service they so desperately need.

Northtown Neighbourhood Advice Centre was awarded Inner Area Partnership funding in 1986 for a period of six years. The central government funding reached the end of its taper in 1992 leaving us reliant on local authority funding. Since then North County Council have provided us with core funding but we have been dependent upon top up funding from charities to maintain this service at full strength. We have established a strategy of fundraising in three year periods. This reduces the time spent on fundraising and enables the Workers to focus on client based work thereby concentrating on providing advice and information and ensuring the project runs smoothly and efficiently. This provides the Centre with the security it needs and ensures continuity of the service to our clients.

We were delighted to move to much larger, more appropriate and accessible premises in December 1997. The premises were afforded to us rent free by a local company which sadly went into receivership this year. We have raised two grants totaling £31,000 to purchase the property in order to retain the service in these premises, which are ideally located. Unlike the previous arrangement we now have additional costs for building insurance, running costs and maintenance.

We expanded the Service in July 2000 by employing a part-time Administration Worker. The Project was keen to employ a person who lived locally and we were fortunate enough to recruit a highly qualified Administration Worker from Northtown who very quickly became an invaluable team member and an integral part of the service. This essential post ensures the smooth running of the project, the continued employment of a local person and allows the Advice Team to focus on advice giving.

Over the past year there has been a significant change in the advice and information sector. The Community Legal Service launched in April 2000 aims to improve access for the public to quality information, advice and specialist legal services. It comprises a set of standards designed to ensure that a service is well run and has its own quality control mechanisms. In anticipation of the application process, the Centre undertook a full internal audit in which we reviewed all practice and procedure. This resulted in further development of the service and a commitment to review the project annually to ensure that we are meeting our clients' needs and maintaining our commitment to quality. The Centre was awarded the quality mark in August 2001.

The enclosed budget for 2002/2003 is based on the last audited accounts for 2000/2001, the actual expenditure for the first six months of 2001/2002 and an estimation of the final six months of 2001/2002 adjusted to take into account a yearly 3% margin for inflation for the year 2002/2003 and for each subsequent year. We have received a grant from the local authority since the Centre opened in 1986 and we therefore feel fairly assured of our core funding over this period (and have assumed a yearly rise of 3%). We have already raised £30,000 (£10,000 per year for 3 years) from the Greggs trust.

We need to raise the amount shown on the attached budget and are applying to a number of funding bodies. If you are unable to award the total amount, a contribution towards it would be invaluable.

We can provide you with copies of our Annual Report and full audited accounts for 2000/2001 if required (we have not automatically enclosed these due to the cost of reproducing them). Please contact us on our ex-directory number if you would like this or any other additional information.

We hope you will treat our application sympathetically and look forward to your reply. Thank you for your help.

Yours sincerely

Alex Janis

PP. B. Matthews

Chair of the Management Committee

However, the application illustrates very well three common mistakes. Firstly, it is unnecessarily downbeat about its financial achievements. It has an excellent history of obtaining and retaining statutory funding. Rather than the slightly negative 'leaving us reliant on local authority funding' it would read much better to say 'we have successfully secured significant, and growing, local authority funding for over ten years [or whatever]'. This is a really good achievement and should be trumpeted. Many organisations are applying effectively to replace lost statutory funding; this one has maintained and developed it.

The application similarly underplays its fundraising success. Again, the negativity of having to secure 'top up funding' could be transformed into outlining how the organisation has developed a range of new initiatives (such as the Community Legal Service) or invested in service delivery (for example through the Administrator). They have successfully fundraised for their own building. All this is very impressive, but doesn't come over that well.

Secondly, the application is confusing about money. In fact, the project has already raised 80% of what it needs, so is a long way down the fundraising road. It should be explicit and upbeat about this. This kind of fundraising success breeds confidence and further success. And this should be clearly stated in the application letter rather than the reader having to look elsewhere to find it.

Thirdly, any application should always state what the money will be used for. If the organisation doesn't want to go down a project fundraising road, and they have a strong track record without having done so, they should still say what are the key areas of service delivery they intend to focus on, or who are the key constituencies. It helps give a feeling that the money will be actively used and that there is on-going direction within the organisation.

And finally, never sign an application pp someone else. It looks as if either you couldn't be bothered or that the application is not sufficiently important to wait until you are next in. Whatever the reason it leaves a really bad impression.

Example 5 – One thing or the other

This is an appeal from a medical research charity. It realises that it is hard to get wide scale company money for straight medical research and so, quite rightly, positions this as a public information campaign. However, once again the appeal makes some major mistakes.

Firstly, and fundamentally, it tries to combine two appeals as one. It asks for support both for the postcards to young people and for the GP/health professionals programme. These are two completely different markets. There are a whole range of companies who would be interested in the youth and student market. Are these companies really also going to be interested in GPs? Aren't these the preserve of drugs manufacturers and other health-orientated companies?

One approach may be to put together a really strong, upbeat proposal about new ways of warning of the dangers of the illness. The postcards could work really well, but should be placed in a positive context. The letter's tone suggests 'Oh, it's all very difficult you know'. Why not take the simple line that if people know what to look out for then half the battle is won? Tell a short story about someone who recognised the symptoms early and therefore received quick, successful treatment.

The company needs to be told what they stand to get out of all of this. Where does the proposed £350 fit into the £150,000 total? Why ask the company to pay 0.2% of the required sum? What good does this do? What recognition will the company get out of this?

Why not put together a formal sponsorship proposal based on the postcards? Presumably there will be thousands printed (although this is not stated) and there will be an effective distribution mechanism. The company's logo could be on each card so would gain it access to a key market. You could even try tying up with a band or night club to get the message better noticed. An alternative to concentrating on the postcards could be to produce a 'wish list' of different publicity options for the company to choose from, each clearly targeted at a particular market.

The GP/health professional leaflet should be an entirely separate proposal, again based on a sponsorship (of the information packs, for example).

Many families in your area have experienced the sudden trauma of ***
over the past year. *** is one of the most dangerous of all medical
conditions, affecting adults and children alike.

*** Charity is the only major UK charity which focuses solely on the funding
of public awareness programmes and vital scientific research as a means
to combat *** and which actively involves families affected by the disease
in its work.

As you may be aware *** is notoriously difficult to diagnose. Yet with early
identification it can often be successfully treated and leaves fewer victims
scarred or disabled by their experience. The *** Charity therefore devotes
a proportion of its resources to raising public awareness of the signs and
symptoms of the disease. There is still a great deal of work that can be
done and I hope [company name] will consider supporting the Charity's
work. I enclose a copy of the Charity's annual review.

The cases of *** have unfortunately been on the increase with young
people. In 1995, there was a two fold percentage rise in notifications of ***
in teenagers and young adults. Currently information resources about
these diseases for young adults are scarce and consequently this winter
the Charity will launch a specific youth orientated initiative. Postcards,
which are currently used to promote bands and night clubs, will be
employed as an accessible medium to promote awareness of the signs and
symptoms of *** to young adults. Once produced, the Postcards will be
distributed to universities, colleges, clubs and restaurants to ensure young
adults can access life saving information on ***.

Another important target group for the winter awareness programme is
GP's and health professionals. We aim through the development and
distribution of new literature to increase understanding of *** that often
accompanies *** and is responsible for the majority of deaths.

To ensure the awareness programme is effective, we need financial
backing. Greater public and professional awareness of *** will save lives. In
the past companies have been very generous with an average donation of
£350. The Foundation is budgeted to spend £150,000 on awareness
programmes during the 1996/97 financial year. If you require any further
information about the awareness campaigns or the research that we are
funding, please do not hesitate to contact me.

I look forward to hearing from you in the near future.

Yours sincerely,

Alan Partridge

Fundraising Officer

Also, the company does not need to know about the gradual improvements in a very difficult medical area. It needs to understand the importance of the problem and that something practical and helpful can be done with its money. The application should describe the PR opportunity rather than simply attempt to sell a medical case.

Finally, there's a strong need for getting an editorial pen to this proposal. Although the above suggestions would change the content quite radically anyway, half the application could effectively be condensed into the following: 'Sadly, the incidence of *** is still on the rise. This is particularly the case with young people (where referrals doubled in 1995). However, the good news is that our researches show that when people can recognise the symptoms, the number of cases is halved (or whatever). We are launching an exciting new initiative to raise awareness about the disease among young people.' The focus could then move onto the postcards, how wonderfully effective they will be in raising awareness and the terrific publicity opportunity they present.

Example 6 – But what difference would we make?

This letter is from a celebrity. It is generally well-written, if a little long-winded. It certainly makes a compelling case, although no doubt some funders would question some of the statistics (is it really true that only 2% of people re-offend? How long after the end of the course were the figures compiled?). Generally the project comes over as being well-run and highly effective. The application contains some basic errors, however, all of which could have been easily avoided.

It's a mail-merged circular. The letter was undated; side two had been pre-printed (including a photocopied signature) onto a roll of computer paper (with the tell-tale perforations top and bottom). So, as a circular it would probably have been binned.

It's a shame that the celebrity didn't actually sign the letter. She is well-known and greatly respected for her community involvement and a personally signed letter from her would give the appeal tremendous weight.

The PS is problematic on two grounds. Firstly, these kinds of PS are best suited to direct mail, and its presence reinforces the impression of a mass mailing rather than a personal letter. Secondly, it suddenly introduces a negative tone, very much out of keeping with the rest of the letter. Why say that the whole future 'is at stake'? It creates doubt in the mind of the donor. If the work is as successful as the letter makes out, there is every reason to assume that the project will go from strength to strength. Try to inspire people to give money, not emotionally bribe or frighten them.

There is also a problem with the way the letter asks for money. Firstly, there is confusion. Are they asking for part of the £500,000 (which is presumably mainly capital expenditure, although this is not clear) or do they want the donor to pay for individual young people at £1,500 a year? They should ask for one or the other, but not both.

In the past you have generously supported the work of *** Foundation, for which we are deeply grateful. Your kindness has allowed over 1,000 people to complete the *** Foundation course, and the results have been remarkable.

I know what it is to plumb the depths of despair. But you don't have to go through what I went through for despair and apathy to take over. Apathy is a problem and it is a killer. It numbs the senses and crushes the spirit. It suffocates self-esteem, blights hope, freezes compassion. Apathy is the product of defeat, and people in our non-functioning inner cities know all about defeat. Many of them are third generation unemployed. Any dreams of success or fulfilment they cherished at school are shattered the moment they leave. Is it any wonder that the first steps to cynicism and alienation start at the school gates.

Almost one million young people are unemployed; 2,874,000 people under 19 live in a household dependent on supplementary benefit and 43% of known offenders are under 21.

You may think this sounds like a lost cause, that the possibility of hauling any young person out of so dire an environment is so slight as to be hopeless. Here at *** Foundation we don't believe in hopelessness, we firmly believe that just because someone has never been given hope it doesn't mean they haven't got any.

A recent survey shows that of the young people who undertook *** Foundation course 42% have found full time employment, 47% have returned to education and 100% undertook a community benefit project. Home Office statistics show that young people who first convict at an early age are more likely to continue offending. 65% of young people had admitted to breaking the law before joining *** and after their involvement with us only 2% have re-offended.

We have shown through the remarkable successes we have had with young people who have undertaken our course, that there is hope and a future for today's youth. Yet there is so much for us still to do – existing centres in *** require expansion to deal with ever-increasing numbers that are being referred to us. New centres need to be established – particularly in ***. Services need to be expanded, but all this requires additional funding.

That is why I am writing to you today, to ask if you will support our national appeal, and raise the £500,000 we need, to give hope and aspiration to more of today's youth.

It costs just £1,500 to fund one young person to go on our course – compare that to the £16,000 a year it costs to keep a young person locked up. A gift of £100 today could radically change the course of a person's life.

The sooner we reach our target, the sooner we can provide the vital work that *** Foundation is renowned for, to communities with high unemployment, high crime and low academic achievement. Please give as much as you can so we can provide a future filled with hope and self-worth for more and more people.

I would like to take this opportunity of wishing you a Happy Christmas, from all the members and staff at *** Foundation, and thank you for your support.

Yours sincerely,

Grace Ellington

PS The enclosed letter from Mary, one of our members sums up in her own words the life of despair she was living before she went on the *** course. The future of young people like Mary and that of *** Foundation is at stake. Please help us to secure both.

If you are going for the £500,000-style approach then you need to have raised some of that total privately before going public (the general rule is get about 25% committed by key donors before opening the appeal up more widely). Give the impression that the appeal has bags of momentum already. Also, you would need to show where the money is coming from and how much you expect trusts, companies or whoever to put in. By breaking everything down into smaller units (say giving yourself a target of £20,000 from companies, £40,000 from trusts, £75,000 from fundraising events etc.), you give the impression that (i) the contribution you are asking for in the letter is much more significant, and (ii) the whole thing is much easier.

Alternatively, if you want £1,500 per person a year, why ask for £100? It doesn't even cover one month's costs. Where does this amount come from? If you are approaching companies, why not set up a friends' scheme whereby they notionally adopt one young person. Or have a corporate members' club whereby you try to recruit W gold members, X silver members, Y bronze members and Z ordinary members. Obviously, the amount each pays comes down as you come down the hierarchy and the benefits you offer increase as you go up. If you are doing this, again you will need to get some members signed up in private first. You need to give the impression in your letter that the company stands to miss out if they don't act now.

Finally, the recipient of this letter had never actually funded the project before. The first line therefore makes a pretty bad impression.

Example 7 – Keep up the momentum

This is a new charity which is clearly meeting a need. The application makes an excellent case, but then rather throws it away at the end. There are various pieces of information that could usefully be added, especially on how many of the 13 million people they are currently helping and how many they plan to help in the future, and what they have done with Lottery funding. However, the basic criticism centres on a very common mistake.

January 2002

Dear Alan

Nearly everyone at some point in their life will experience the terrifying symptoms of an anxiety/panic attack. F.U.S.E., a new organisation, has been established to help people who find themselves in this terrifying situation and it has received official recognition by both the Charity Commission and the National Lottery Charities Board.

There are an estimated 13 million people in the UK who are enduring complicated anxiety based problems such as panic attacks, phobias and obsessive/compulsive disorders. Often sufferers are too ill or afraid to leave their homes and whilst this affects anyone, anywhere, it is especially a dilemma for people in rural areas where there is little or no quick access to local support. You may, or may not, know that the highest rate of suicide occurs amongst farming communities. People, young and old, who live in small villages, are often extremely isolated and this is not conducive to recovery from an anxiety disorder. We are able to help by running Recovery Groups on a teleconference network. A course covers 14 weeks using cognitive and behavioral therapy with a further opportunity to participate in a befriending group afterwards. This helps to establish and support recovery. Also, group members are encouraged to take an active part in the running of the charity by being trained to act as Group Leaders themselves, consequently furthering their own knowledge and helping more fellow sufferers.

Unfortunately, anxiety illnesses know no boundaries and it is apparent that the services F.U.S.E. can provide are becoming an essential commodity in these stressful times. Our charity is totally non-profit making and volunteer based and we are hoping that you will be able to offer financial support to enable this new and forward-looking project to flourish and grow. We are determined to do our best to make this happen and hope you will help.

Yours sincerely

Samantha Taylor

CHAIRPERSON

The application flags up a compelling issue – in this case the high incidence of anxiety illnesses in rural areas – which really grabs the reader's interest. But then it more or less immediately moves away from it and tails off into a generalised 'please help'.

This is, or should be, an excellent example of project fundraising. Anxiety-based illnesses are clearly a wide-ranging problem and a particular need in rural areas. There is a viable solution on offer, although it needs explaining in more detail. It would seem perfectly natural, therefore, for the application to finish off by simply stating how much this rural work currently costs and how much money they need to develop it further.

It should be fairly straightforward to raise the money needed. This is a newish organisation with a quickly established track record. It simply needs to follow through the argument it begins to develop, and have the confidence to ask for what it actually needs. Remember, fundraising is about change, not money. The case for change is half made, and could easily be fully made. The case for money then flows perfectly naturally.

Examples 8 and 9 – Building on a local connection

Not every donor will be interested in your work. This is particularly true for local projects seeking support from a company where there almost always needs to be a local connection.

Example 8 was an obviously circular letter, with the addressee written in by hand at the top of the page. It is short and clearly laid out – so far, so good. But the writer makes a number of assumptions – that Kodak (based in Hemel Hempstead) has an interest in improving the living conditions of a Sheffield community; that Kodak could somehow 'improve its profile' by investing in community development; and lastly, that Kodak can make a significant contribution to a very large budget.

This is a typical letter where an applicant has not understood – or even bothered to find out about – the grants policies of the donor, and has simply assumed that because the charity is short of money a large company would be interested in giving it.

To R Miller of Kodak Ltd from the Chairman of Eastside Community Association/Action Group

Dear Sir,

I am writing to you on behalf of the above mentioned voluntary organisation.

Eastside is a rapidly developing Community situated on the boundary of Sheffield and whose village services are at present under immense strain. To overcome the problem the Action Group was formed with a view to developing a new Community Centre based on the conversion of the now vacant local Vicarage.

A project report showing an Architects proposed design and costings for the scheme is enclosed for your perusal.

The self help group now need the backing for this Centre which is badly needed to provide facilities especially for the under 5s and senior citizens. We need a total of £196,000, and are looking for financial support from your good selves for which we in return can enlarge your company profile and market awareness in a rapidly developing new township.

Obviously any help in this project would be gratefully received and any conditions imposed on sponsorship we would endeavor to meet.

However we must emphasise the urgency of our request and look forward to receiving your early reply.

Thanking you in anticipation.

Yours faithfully,

Richard Fuller

The second letter, from Hammersmith and Fulham Amenity Trust (example 9), recognises the importance of the local connection and uses an opportunity from the company chairman's publicly-stated concern to start the grants process moving. Because the company is a very large local employer with long historic ties in the borough, the trust is obviously seeking a large grant. To this end, the first step is to build a relationship, rather than ask for a donation. The letter is the first step; then a phone call; then, hopefully, a meeting to discuss how the trust and the company might work in partnership; and only then, an application for support.

To Richard Fuller, Public Relations Manager of Fuller Smith and Turner from the Director of the Hammersmith and Fulham Amenity Trust

Dear Mr Fuller

UK2000 Thames Project – Environmental Improvements

I noted with pleasure that your chairman, Mr Anthony Fuller, represented Fullers at the UK2000 reception aboard the Elizabethan recently on July 28th, as it demonstrated your company's obvious concern for the environment. I am aware of your company's long association with our part of London, particularly the river, and in view of this I hope that we will be able to link up with you in some of our environmental projects.

Hammersmith and Fulham Amenity Trust was established in 1982 to make our borough a brighter and greener place to visit, work or live in and to create training and employment opportunities. The Trust is an independent charity which receives support from a variety of public and private bodies and carries out a wide range of work including landscape gardening, tree planting, and playgrounds combined with our training schemes for local unemployed people, and events such as the Thames Project. Our newsletter, annual report and other publications are designed to inform the public on green issues and promote a better environment.

Our work is initiated by individuals and groups representing residents, schools, housing associations, playgroups, local businesses, health authorities and the Council – all our projects involve local people in their design, implementation and maintenance after completion.

Currently we have a number of projects which your company may wish to support ranging from improvements to the riverside and canalside, to greening some of the borough's bleaker housing estates, a garden for a home for the elderly, a children's play area, tree and bulb planting in several locations.

I hope that your company would like to take the opportunity that the Trust presents to become more closely associated with improving the quality of our environment and I will contact you shortly to discuss further details.

Yours sincerely,

R. Miller

(annual report and newsletter enclosed)

Example 10 – Stressing the benefits

With a sponsorship application, the company is interested in the benefits it will receive if it gives its support.

This letter sets out the benefits quite clearly – including the hidden benefit of doing something in ASDA's patch. Tesco, as a company, is promoting its healthy, caring and environmentally sound image. This project could fit well into this strategy.

However, the benefits as stated in this application have not really been quantified. How many people will visit the show? How much local publicity and press coverage will be generated? What other ways of meeting Tesco's needs are possible (for example, giving out discount vouchers to encourage people to visit the store)? An organisation seeking sponsorship should think carefully about the benefits, be as specific as possible and then see whether it is possible to make the proposition even more attractive to a potential sponsor.

To the Manager of the local Tesco Stores from a member of the Voluntary Management Committee of Northtown City Farm

Dear Mr Garbutt,

I am writing to offer you the opportunity of sponsoring an event at Northtown City Farm, a local project with which many of your staff and customers are no doubt familiar. I had originally approached ASDA as their Northtown store is just down the road from the Farm, but they have chosen to turn down a chance of gaining good publicity for themselves.

Northtown City Farm is an ambitious voluntary community project providing considerable social, recreational and educational benefits to local people in a whole range of activities extending way beyond the central farmyard. We cater for people of all ages, as you will see from the enclosed leaflet and Annual Report.

Many of our members (over 800 families) and local poultry breeders are pressing us to put on a Poultry Show, which we would like to do one Saturday in September if we can obtain financial support for it. I believe your Company would derive much benefit from sponsoring this event for several reasons.

1) Tesco would be able to promote its products and the local store by advertising at the show.

2) Tesco would enhance its caring image through its partnership with a popular community project enjoyed by hundreds of adults and children living in the area around the Brislington store.

3) Tesco would earn respect for joining with us in our efforts to bring a greater understanding of farming to city people. Many of our potential exhibitors are keen to show their poultry in the city for the same reason.

Our estimated costs for putting on the show (including hire of equipment, transport, publicity, judges expenses, prize money, staffing, insurance and other overheads) are £1,420. We are confident of the Show's success because of the interest already being shown and the enthusiasm of small local breeders who feel unable to show their birds at large agricultural shows but would welcome an opportunity to participate in a smaller event.

I should be delighted if Tesco Stores agreed to sponsor this year's event. You are very welcome to come and visit the Farm, and I would be pleased to answer any questions you may have. I look forward to hearing from you.

Yours sincerely,

Paula Ironside

11 Assessing your Application

Few applications are perfect, even the ones that raise lots of money. Most can be significantly improved, and it is surprising how many miss out something of real importance.

Before you send off your application, it's worth checking it thoroughly, not just for spelling mistakes, but to make sure that all the details are correct and that you haven't missed out your key selling point or a vital piece of information.

This chapter aims to help you assess:

- How good is your application?
- How, if at all, might you improve it?

Have you written a good application?

Style

✔ **The title**: is the project title succinct, catchy, appropriate?

✔ **First paragraph**: does the first paragraph grab the reader's attention, create sufficient interest for the reader to continue with the proposal?

✔ **Writing**: are you happy with the way you have written this proposal? Does it read well?

✔ **Length**: is it the right length? Does it include all the key points you wish to make?

✔ **Tone**: is the proposal positive, confident, enthusiastic? Does it create a sense of urgency and importance for the project?

✔ **Logical flow**: is there a logical structure to the proposal going from problem to solution, from solution to the resources required to provide that solution, and from the resources you require to how the donor can help?

✔ **Visual impression**: is the proposal nicely laid-out with shortish paragraphs, sub-heads and tabulations (where appropriate)? Is it typed neatly and without spelling mistakes?

✔ **Letterhead**: are you happy with your organisation's letterhead? Is it visually attractive? Does it contain all the information it should?

Communication with the donor

✔ **Personal approach**: does the application give the impression of being a personal letter individually written to the donor? Is it signed personally?

✔ **Previous contact**: does the application mention previous approaches or any other contacts you may have had with the donor?

✔ **Donor interests**: is the proposal likely to be of interest to the donor, knowing what you do about their concerns and priorities?

✔ **Donor guidelines**: if the donor publishes guidelines for applicants, have you read these carefully, and does your application fall clearly within the guidelines?

✔ **Scale of request**: is your request reasonable, given what you know about the donor's scale of grant-making?

✔ **Rationale**: have you given good reasons why the donor should want to support the project? If writing to a company, have you clearly stated the benefits they will get from supporting you?

✔ **Empathy**: are you on the same wavelength as the donor? Or, if you are not, does the application build a bridge between your point of view and theirs?

✔ **Signatory**: is the signatory to the letter the most appropriate for the particular donor? And is he or she the first point of contact?

✔ **Follow up**: do you suggest any follow up if the proposal is of particular interest (a site visit, the supply of further and more detailed information, a meeting)?

✔ **Report back**: if you are seeking substantial support, do you indicate how and at what intervals you intend to report on progress?

...or a bad application?

Style

✗ **First paragraph**: is the first paragraph a turn off? Will the reader lose interest and read no further?

✗ **Writing**: is it dreary, verbose and stuffed with jargon, unsubstantiated superlatives, long sentences and unnecessarily long words?

✗ **Length**: is it over-long? Can you shorten it by cutting out unnecessary words? Have you tried to say too much?

✗ **Tone**: is the tone of the proposal hectoring or over-assertive? Is it whinging or apologetic? Or is it complacent?

✗ **Logical flow**: is the application a complete muddle? Do you dart from one point to another and back again? Do you repeat yourself?

✗ **Visual impression**: is the typing a mess? Are there spelling mistakes? Does it contain great chunks of unbroken text?

✗ **Letterhead**: have you got a massive letterhead which takes up half a page? Does it include out-of-date information (e.g. names of trustees who have moved on, are no longer MPs or whatever)? Is there any other problem with it?

Communication with the donor

✗ **Personal approach**: is the application a circular appeal? Does it give the impression of having been sent off to a large number of people (whether or not this is actually the case)?

✗ **Previous contact**: have you failed to mention any previous contact (even if you were turned down)?

✗ **Donor interests**: does the proposal fall completely outside the donor's known concerns and priorities? If so, why are you writing to them (you must have a really good reason)?

✗ **Donor guidelines**: have you forgotten to get hold of the guidelines? Have you not really read them, or deliberately misinterpreted them so that you fit in?

✗ **Scale of request**: does the scale of your need and your request fail to match the scale of the donor's grant-making? Are you looking for such a large sum that the donor can't really make a worthwhile contribution? Conversely, are you looking for such a small sum that the donor can't really be bothered?

✗ **Rationale**: do you just hope the donor may be interested, that by a process of osmosis they will understand the benefits of their support?

✗ **Empathy**: are you too radical or not radical enough, too establishment or not establishment enough, on the wrong network or wavelength?

✗ **Signatory**: has the application letter been signed by the fundraising assistant, or signed pp by the signatory's secretary? Does this give the impression that you can't really be bothered?

✗ **Report back**: will they next hear from you when you next want money?

Have you written a good application?

Content

✔ **Need**: have you made a good case (centred on your users) and supported it with a few relevant facts and figures?

✔ **Credibility**: have you established that your organisation has the ability, the particular skills and the other resources necessary to make an impact?

✔ **The proposal**: have you explained in clear, simple terms exactly what you propose to do? Is it backed up by evidence? Is everything the donor needs to know included in the letter?

✔ **Project idea**: is the project likely to be seen as interesting, relevant, attractive to a donor? Does it have the support of users? Will it bring measurable benefits to the lives of your users?

✔ **Objectives**: have you set yourself specific and measurable objectives for the project? And are these reasonable given the level of staff time and resources at your disposal? Are you confident?

✔ **Evaluation**: do you intend to evaluate the outcome of your work and have you shown how you intend to set about doing this? Is this likely to be effective and is it being done at reasonable cost?

✔ **Dissemination**: if the proposal is for a pilot project, for research or action research, or to produce a publication, have you shown how you plan to disseminate the results, or what you have produced with the grant?

✔ **The offer**: have you made a specific request for support or given a clear indication to the donor as to how much you want them to give? Have you mentioned where the rest of the money is coming from, or who has already given to the appeal?

✔ **Future funding**: have you at least shown that you have thought about the future funding implications of the proposal (the running costs, or whatever) even though there may be no certain answers at this stage?

Budget

✔ **Arithmetic**: do the figures add up?

✔ **Costings**: have you included all the items of expenditure that you plan to incur? Are all the items costed realistically?

✔ **Overheads**: where appropriate, have you included an apportionment of overhead of administrative costs in your budget? Does the basis on which you have calculated this appear reasonable?

✔ **Value**: does the total cost appear to you to be reasonable in relation to the work you plan to do? Does the proposal represent value for the donor's money? Is this clear from what you have said?

✔ **Inflation**: if the project is to run over several years, have you made any allowance for inflation (or stated that the budget for future years does not take account of any inflation in costs)?

Supporting information

✔ **Finance**: have you included your annual accounts and a budget for the project?

✔ **Brochure**: have you got a suitable brochure or report to attach? Does it enhance what you say in the application? Is it nicely designed and illustrated?

✔ **Other**: is there any other information you could or should include?

...or a bad application?

Content

✗ **Need**: have you simply assumed that everyone knows what you are doing is important? Have you spoken in generalisations and made bland assertions?

✗ **Credibility**: have you assumed that everybody has heard about you, thinks well of you, and is convinced of your capabilities?

✗ **Proposal**: is your description of the project muddled? Incomplete? Are you expecting the donor to wade through loads of supporting material to get a proper idea of what you are trying to do.

✗ **Project idea**: have you made the project seem boring, old-fashioned, of marginal benefit?

✗ **Objectives**: have you failed to set objectives? Are they very generalised, couched in 'We hope this...' or 'We may do...'? Or are the objectives so grandiose that they become completely unrealistic?

✗ **Dissemination**: are you keeping everything to yourselves?

✗ **The offer**: have you mentioned some global fundraising target and simply asked for 'a generous contribution'? Have you given no indication of the scale of support you are looking for?

✗ **Future funding**: are you asking for running costs and giving no indication of how the project will continue in future years? Are you asking for an item of equipment or raising money for a building, without giving any indication of how the running costs will be met?

Budget

✗ **Arithmetic**: are there silly mistakes in your addition?

✗ **Costings**: have you forgotten to include certain items of expenditure? Are the figures just 'plucked out of the air'? Have you obtained any quotes or estimates for larger items of capital expenditure?

✗ **Value**: does the proposal seem a lot of money for what you plan to do?

Supporting information

✗ **Brochure**: is your supporting material written for internal consumption (as, say, a discussion document)? Is it written in long paragraphs, no sub heads, heavily jargonised? Is it overly glossy or does it look too cheap?

Assessing your application

Now assess your application on the following lines:

Factor	Satisfied?	Action points
Style	Yes/no	
Title		
First paragraph		
Writing		
Length		
Tone		
Logical flow		
Visual impression		
Letterhead		
Communication with donor	Yes/no	
Personal approach		
Previous contact		
Donor interests		
Donor guidelines		
Scale of request		
Rationale		
Empathy		
Signatory		
Follow up		
Report back		

Factor	Satisfied?	Action points
Content	Yes/no	
Need		
Credibility		
Proposal		
Project idea		
Objectives		
Evaluation		
Dissemination		
The offer		
Future funding		
Budget	Yes/no	
Arithmetic		
Costings		
Overheads		
Value for money		
Inflation		
Supporting information	Yes/no	
Finance		
Brochure		
Other		

CHECKLISTS AND FACT FILES

Serious fundraising requires serious record-keeping. Much of this involves getting information that is dispersed throughout the organisation (or lives only in people's heads) and putting it into a central file. This can be time-consuming. However, once you have done it (and as long as you keep updating it as you go) it is a fairly straightforward maintenance job.

The information you keep is entirely up to you. The following covers the various points and issues discussed in this book. Use it or adapt it as necessary.

Contents

1 Organisation fact file

The basic facts about your organisation, its aims and its history. Often this is forgotten.

2 Credibility fact file

Some basic information about the successes and achievements of the organisation, its main financial sponsors (whose support provides an endorsement) and note of any recent press and media coverage.

3 Credibility box file

A box file in which you keep endorsements; quotations; lists of patrons and financial sponsors; clippings from newspaper articles or research reports highlighting the problem or need; statistics and trends which demonstrate the full extent of the problem and how the situation is changing; evaluation reports which reflect the good work being done by the organisation; case studies and photographs that put a human face on your work; in fact anything that might be useful in reinforcing your case. Every organisation should have one!

4 Fundraising plan for the organisation

To help you plan your fundraising needs well in advance.

5 Project fact file

The basic facts about your project, its importance and how it will be run.

6 Budget checklist

To help you plan your expenditure requirements.

7 Fundraising plan for the project

To help you plan where and how you will raise the money you need for your project, and to develop contingency plans if you are not immediately successful.

8 Keeping track of progress

Checklists to record the grants and donations you receive and to track the progress of your more important applications.

9 Mobilising contacts

To help you identify the personal contacts and mobilise the support of your staff, trustees, patrons and others who can help you in your fundraising.

1 Organisation fact file

Last updated:

Name of your organisation:

Address:

Date founded:

Why, how and by whom founded:

Key events in your organisation's history (up to 5):

Charitable status:

    Registration or reference no:

    If not a charity, describe status of the organisation:

    VAT registration no:

People involved

    numbers of full time staff: numbers of part time staff:
    numbers of volunteers: volunteer hours a year:
    individual membership: institutional membership:

Annual income

    total income:
    total raised from grants and donations:
    total self-generated:
    total expenditure:
    total assets:

Mission statement:

Principal objects or purposes of the organisation:

Present policies and priorities:

Business plan last updated in:

Beneficial area or area over which the organisation operates:

Affiliations with other relevant organisations:

The organisation: what makes it unique or different and why its work is especially important (3 key facts):

Recent growth in the organisation and in the demand for its services (3 key statistics):

2 Credibility fact file

Last updated:

List your five greatest successes in the past five years:

Other recent successes and achievements of the organisation (2 or 3):

Main financial sponsors:
  - government and other official sources:

  - grant-making trusts:

  - business sponsors:

  - individual supporters:

  - prominent patrons and supporters:

Recent press or media coverage:

3 Credibility box file

This is simply where you keep all the press coverage, statements, quotations, evaluations or other information about the organisation which endorse the value of its work. Once it's full, start pruning the out-of-date clippings.

4 A fundraising plan for the organisation

Fundraising always takes time, and it is sensible to plan well ahead. Ideally draw up a three or five-year budget of income and expenditure. The following is a suggestion for an income budget in order to plan your fundraising (an expenditure budget in this book would be so generalised as to be useless).

Start by looking at your income and expenditure over the last four or five years. Do you notice any trends (e.g. rise in salary or premises costs; fall in local authority grant; growth in income from grant-making trusts; increasing reliance on one source of income)? Make a note of them and make sure your fundraising plan takes full account of them. For example, if you have never had any company sponsorship, it will take time to build this up. Don't put £100,000 down in year one just because it looks good.

When compiling your figures, make a note of any assumptions and action points, particularly with regard to large chunks of income. Also, remember that this exercise is, at best, a guesstimate. You cannot guarantee future income, so if it appears you have got your projections wrong, change them.

Finally, be honest and realistic! The temptation is to write up income and write down expenditure, when it is more often the other way round.

Here are some possible budget headings you might use for your income projections.

Total budgeted or estimated expenditure for the year £ _____

Income to be raised (*by category*)

Investment income and bank interest £ _____

Earned income from:

contracts for service delivery £ _____

other sale of services £ _____

training & conferences £ _____

publication sales £ _____

other trading activities £ _____

Grants/payments from:

central government £ _____

local government £ _____

other statutory sources £ _____

trusts £ _____

National Lottery £ _____

company donations £ _____

business sponsorship £ _____

other sources £ _____

Public fundraising

    membership subscriptions   £ _____

    fundraising events   £ _____

    Gift Aid/planned giving   £ _____

    collections   £ _____

    other   £ _____

Legacies   £ _____

Total income budgeted for the year   £ _____

Budgeted surplus or deficit   £ _____

Comments

Key dates:

    schedule of expiring grants:

        larger grants which are likely to be renewed (list sources/annual amount/expiry date/renewal action to be taken and by whom/comments)

        larger grants which are unlikely to be renewed (list sources/annual amount/expiry date/suggestions for alternative sources of funding/comments)

    schedule of expiring contracts/service agreements:

        major contracts/service agreements which are likely to be renewed

        major contracts/service agreements which are unlikely to be renewed

    key fundraising events (timetable for who is doing what and by when)

    covenant/Gift Aid tax reclaim (who does it by when)

5 Project fact file

This brings together information about the project you are raising money for

Last updated:

Description of the proposed project/purpose of the application (not more than 20 words):

The need for the project – 3 key facts:

Evidence that users believe that there is a need.

Partner organisations (how and why are they involved):

Why it is so important to undertake the project at the present time (3 key points):

The objective (main aim) of the project:

How and when will the above objective come about (specific and measurable outputs)?

Methods which will be used to undertake the project:

Up to five key tasks you will undertake in the first year:

User involvement: how will the users be involved in the work?

Volunteer inputs: how are volunteers to be involved and what is the value of this?

How do you plan to disseminate any results or the outcome of the project?

How will the project will be evaluated?

Any consequences or anticipated future impact which will result from the project:

Estimated start date of the project:

Estimated completion date or term of the project:

Key people involved and relevant experience:

Outside advisers:

Any other details of the project which are particularly special or noteworthy:

6 Budget checklist – revenue project

Here is an outline budget for a revenue project. We have left space at the bottom for two subsequent revisions, the first in the light of your assessment of the fundraising potential of the project (you may wish to increase or reduce certain costs, or add to or subtract from the project), and the second to allow you to confirm or get better estimates for the major items of cost.

Project title:

1st draft

	Year 1	Year 2	Year 3
Employment costs/salaries (inc. National Insurance)	....	....	....
Recruitment costs	....	....	....
Volunteer expenses/ training costs	....	....	....
Project costs			
Equipment	....	....	....
Printing/stationery	....	....	....
Post/telephone	....	....	....
Travel/transport	....	....	....
Training	....	....	....
Evaluation	....	....	....
Technical advice/ consultancy	....	....	....
Dissemination of results	....	....	....
Other project costs	....	....	....
	....	....	....
	....	....	....

	Year 1	Year 2	Year 3
Overhead costs *			
Office occupancy (rent/rates/heat/ light etc.)	....	....	....
Management & administration	....	....	....
Central services (cleaning etc.)	....	....	....
Depreciation	....	....	....
Other overhead costs	....	....	....
	....	....	....
	....	....	....
TOTAL	£.....................	£.....................	£.....................

* State basis on which overhead costs have been apportioned to the project

State basis on which inflation has been allowed for in the second and third years

State any other relevant assumptions

		Year 1	Year 2	Year 3
First revision	TOTAL	....	....	....
Second revision	TOTAL	....	....	....

7 Fundraising plan for the project

Just as you will need an income budget for the organisation, you will also need budgets for each of the projects that the organisation undertakes as part of its work. Having costed the project – (*see Checklist 6 Budget checklist*), you will need to draw up an income budget. You will need a separate column for each year of the project.

Firstly, categorise the budgeted income under the different heads:

- government and other statutory sources
- grant-making trusts and other charities
- business support (inc. sponsorship and gifts in kind)
- donations from members/individual supporters
- fundraising events and activities
- your organisation's own contribution
- other

Under each income source, you will need to list:

- total income to be raised from that source
- a list of grants raised or committed to date, and a total for this committed income
- a list of likely grants still being negotiated or decided, and a total for this probable income
- the total income still required
- any notes or comments

Compare your *Fundraising plan for the project* with *Checklist 4 A Fundraising plan for the organisation*. For example, are you aiming to raise the entire trust's budget for a single project? If so, (i) is this realistic, and (ii) what about the other projects you are trying to raise money for?

You will need to keep your project plan up-to-date, recording grants when they come in and revising estimates and running totals accordingly. Where you fail to secure a major grant which you had been planning for, you may need to revise your whole approach. A contingency plan can alert you to the possibilities.

8 Keeping track of progress

You need to keep track of the progress of each key grant you have applied for. In the light of this, review the situation regularly and take action sooner rather than later. If you don't, you may end up with a large hole in your budget. For each grant, keep the following information:

Who you applied to

How much you asked for/expect

Name of person you sent it to

Who signed the letter

Date application was sent off

Expected decision date

Follow up action:

    (i) action already taken

    (ii) the possibilities of further action

    (iii) suggestions for possible alternative sources

Person responsible for negotiating the grant

9 Mobilising contacts

You can improve your chances significantly by developing good personal contacts with the trustees and others responsible for grants decisions in the bodies you are approaching. This section provides an 'audit' of the contacts that you, your colleagues, your trustees and your patrons already have as a start to mobilising their support. Remember too that your employee volunteers can be particularly important when approaching their employer.

For each of your colleagues, your trustees, your patrons, and possibly even some of your key supporters and most committed volunteers, keep a record of the following information.

Name

Position/occupation

Contact address/phone/fax/e-mail

Any relevant skills they have and help they are prepared to give

Useful contacts they are prepared to approach for support (or let you approach on their behalf)

Name/position/address/telephone of the contact

Funding body and their connection with it

Whether you or they will make the approach

Notes (e.g. what is the existing relationship with this contact/funding body)

The help you will want from your supporters will be anything from:

- Sounding the funder out
- Having a quiet, informal word over dinner
- Attending (or even making) a formal presentation of your project to the funder
- Signing a covering letter
- Asking formally for money face to face

For further information see Data Protection for voluntary organisations, Paul Ticher, published by DSC.

FURTHER READING AND SOURCES OF INFORMATION

About the Directory of Social Change

The Directory of Social Change (DSC) is an independent voice for positive social change, set up in 1975 to help voluntary organisations become more effective. It does this by providing practical, challenging and affordable information and training to meet the current, emerging and future needs of the sector.

DSC's main activities include:

- researching and publishing reference guides and handbooks;
- providing practical training courses;
- running conferences and briefing sessions;
- organising Charityfair, the biggest annual forum for the sector;
- encouraging voluntary groups to network and share information;
- campaigning to promote the interests of the voluntary sector as a whole.

Contact addresses and telephone numbers for all departments can be found at the start of this book, opposite the Contents page.

Books available from DSC

The following is a selection of titles available by mail order from the Publications department. Telephone 020 7209 5151 or e-mail books@dsc.org.uk for a complete catalogue, or visit the DSC website: www.dsc.org.uk

Editions and prices were correct at the time of going to press but may be subject to change.

Directories

A Guide to the Major Trusts, Vol. 1: the top 300 trusts (making grants annually of over £300,000 a year), DSC, 2001, £19.95

A Guide to the Major Trusts Vol. 2: the next 700 trusts (making grants annually of over £60,000 a year), DSC, 2001, £19.95

A Guide to the Major Trusts Vol. 3: the next 500 trusts (making grants annually of over £20,000 a year), DSC, 2002, £17.95

A Guide to Scottish Trusts: details of 350 trusts which concentrate their grantmaking in Scotland, DSC, 2002, £16.95

A Guide to Local Trusts: four volumes covering local trusts in the North of England, the Midlands, The South of England and Greater London, DSC, 2002, £17.95

The Grant-making Trusts CD-ROM (all the trusts from the CAF and DSC databases on one CD-ROM), developed by FunderFinder for DSC, 2002, £110 + VAT

Website: *www.trustfunding.org.uk* contains all the same data as the *Grant-making Trusts CD-ROM*, but is regularly updated throughout the year.

The Educational Grants Directory, DSC, Sarah Wiggins and Dave Griffiths, 7th edition 2002, c. £19.95

A Guide to Grants for Individuals in Need, Sarah Wiggins and Dave Griffiths, 8th edition 2002, c. £19.95

The Guide to UK Company Giving, John Smyth, DSC, 4th edition 2002, £25

The CD-ROM Company Giving Guide, developed by FunderFinder for DSC, 3rd edition 2002, £50 + VAT

Funding guides and handbooks

The Complete Fundraising Handbook, Nina Botting and Michael Norton, DSC in association with the Institute of Fundraising, 4th edition 2001, £16.95

The Arts Funding Guide, Susan Forrester and David Lloyd, DSC, 6th edition 2002, c.£16.95

The Schools Funding Guide, Nicola Eastwood, Anne Mountfield and Louise Walker, DSC, 2001, £16.95

The Sports Funding Guide, Nicola Eastwood, DSC in association with Sport England, 2nd edition 1999, £16.95

The Youth Funding Guide, Nicola Eastwood, DSC, 2nd edition 2002, £16.95

'How to' guides

Building a Fundraising Database Using Your PC, DSC/CAF, Peter Flory, 2nd edition, 2001, £12.95

Find the Funds, Christopher Carnie, DSC/CAF, 1st edition, 2000, £12.95

Fundraising from Grant-making Trusts and Foundations, Karen Gilchrist & Margo Horsley, DSC/CAF 1st edition, 2000, £10.95

Looking After Your Donors, Karen Gilchrist, DSC/CAF, 1st edition, 2000, £10.95

Organising Special Events, John F Gray & Stephen Elsden, DSC/CAF, 1st edition, 2001, £10.95

Promoting Your Cause, Karen Gilchrist, DSC/CAF, 1st edition, 2002, £10.95

Training available from DSC

For a copy of the latest training guide, contact the training department on 020 7391 4808, e-mail training@dsc.org.uk or visit the DSC website: www.dsc.org.uk